zen

GARDENING

zen

GARDENING

VERONICA RAY

BERKLEY BOOKS, NEW YORK

ZEN GARDENING

A Berkley Book / published by arrangement with
the author

PRINTING HISTORY
Berkley trade paperback edition / June 1996

The Putnam Berkley World Wide Web site address is
http://www.berkley.com

ISBN: 0-425-15299-5

BERKLEY®
Berkley Books are published by The Berkley Publishing Group,
200 Madison Avenue, New York, New York 10016.
BERKLEY and the "B" design
are trademarks belonging to Berkley Publishing Corporation.

PRINTED IN THE UNITED STATES OF AMERICA

10   9   8   7   6   5   4   3   2   1

CONTENTS

INTRODUCTION

The enjoyments of a garden being so manifold and continuous, bringing brightness to the home, health to the body, and happiness to the mind, it is for us, who have proved them, whose daily lives are made more cheerful by their influence, to invite and instruct others, that they may share our joy.

—S. Reynolds Hole

This book is not intended as an instruction, but an invitation to the abundant joys of gardens and gardening, and to the peaceful joy of Zen. I am neither an expert gardener nor a Zen master. I am just someone who has a deep love for both. I try to be open to what they can each show me. I read and listen to all the so-called experts and take what I can use, but I know that my own experience is the best teacher, as long as I am open to learning and having what I think I already know disproven.

It's called *beginner's mind*—an openness to the joys of experience, of learning, of life. I have no intention or desire to end up at some point where I will call myself an expert in either gardening or Zen. If I did, I would have to give them up and find some other way to learn new things. The idea is to always remain in beginner's mind. When we do that, there is no end to the lessons we can learn.

Zen is not a dogmatic religion or philosophy, but simply a practice. And yet, for all of our practice, we are rewarded with powerful insight and a deep, peaceful joy. The garden is the perfect setting in which to practice Zen. It presents us with lessons in patience, compassion, and acceptance—all aspects of the Zen viewpoint. It teaches us awareness, simplicity, nonattachment, nonresistance, our interdependence and interconnectedness with all life, and present-moment living. It gives us the opportunity to lose ourselves in mindful, attentive work.

Any garden can be a Zen garden. While Zen monks slowly, carefully, and deliberately rake fields of pebbles or sand into perfect patterns and call them Zen gardens, we can call any plot of land, window box, or backyard a Zen garden. It does not matter what the garden looks like; what matters is how we garden there; how we interact with it; how we feel, think, and behave in it. Zen is a practice, and when we practice Zen and gardening at the same time, the results are many lessons learned and much joy created.

In Zen, we learn to live one moment at a time, one breath at a time, right here and right now. We learn to trust the energy of the universe, the perfect nature of all nature. We feel our oneness with all other beings and the earth we share. We perform our work mindfully, attentively, and deliberately. We lose ourselves in the energy that flows through us and everything else. In gardening, we learn to let nature know best, to accept what we can't control, and to become a harmonious and helpful part of nature's process. We become one with the natural world, letting it work through us.

If you are a gardener who is unfamiliar with Zen, you can discover a new approach to your gardening that will deepen and enrich your gardening experience. If you are a Zen practitioner who has never gardened before, you can discover a great new method of practice. If you have been a stranger to both Zen and gardening, a whole new wonderful world awaits you.

This book is a kind of diary; it contains thoughts I've had in and about my garden and lessons I have learned from it. The garden is a metaphor for everything else in life, and all of life's important lessons can be learned there. Zen is a way of opening ourselves up to learning those lessons. It's a new way of approaching, interacting, and communicating with our gardens. It's a practice of slowing down, paying attention, and being fully present there. When Zen and gardening meet, our flowers and vegetables, trees and shrubs, hearts, minds, and spirits all blossom together in a rainbow of brilliant color. May all your gardens be bountiful.

PLANNING MY GARDEN

Of all human activities, apart from the procreation of children, gardening is the most optimistic and hopeful. The gardener is by definition one who plans for and believes and trusts in the future, whether in the short or the longer term.

—Susan Hill

To make a great garden, one must have a great idea or a great opportunity.

—Sir George Sitwell

There are many ways of spending one's money in gardening but the most tempting, at least to me, occurs with the arrival of the bulb catalogues.

—Christopher Lloyd

Life begins the day you start a garden.

—Chinese proverb

A window in my office, where I write, looks out on my garden. Today it is barren. The deck and fence have yet to be painted. The barrier fencing between the deck and the yard has yet to be built. The raised beds brimming with lush vegetable plants and the lattice arbor covered with vines and flowers are still only images in my mind. It is April. The birds, ducks, and geese are back, busy building their nests and families. The snow has long since melted into the absorbent earth. The air is fresh and cool, filled with promise.

In the early spring, I start receiving lots of gardening catalogs in the mail. I spend many hours poring over them, fantasizing about this year's garden. I imagine the colors, scents, textures, and visual appeal of hundreds of flower varieties. I plot a vegetable garden, overflowing with fresh produce to grow, pick, and eat, all within a space of ten feet. I draw aerial pictures of my property, putting in a variety of optional plantings, fences, fountains, benches, raised beds, and pots. In my mind, my garden comes alive in various stages of growth and work, various configurations of design.

I find an infinite source of ideas in books filled with photographs of gardens all over the world. I fill my mind with these images, adapting both their essences and their practical aspects to my own space and conditions. The feeling of a cool, dark maze in the English countryside finds its way into an arbor over a bench in a shady corner of my backyard. The peace and gentleness of a Japanese meditation garden reveals itself in clean, simple lines of geometric raised beds and walkways. The brilliant shock of a field of California poppies springs into a colorful bed of perennial and annual flowers.

All of this plotting and planning fills the last days of gray skies, cold temperatures, and barren landscapes with the fire of abundance to come. I can try hundreds of variations before deciding on anything, spending any money, or picking up a shovel. I can rehearse my summer's work and enjoy its results and rewards without ever leaving my armchair. My pleasure in this year's garden begins in the cool early spring, in the fertile soil of my mind. All of this thinking, reading, planning, and plotting is also an integral part of the garden itself. It comes into existence in my imagination before a single seed is planted. Its energy begins gathering and creating momentum that will carry it through the entire season. Its life has begun long before the first truly warm day of the year.

It's like planning a trip. A big part of the enjoyment, the true *pleasure* of traveling is studying the places we might go, plotting our route and the things we'll do and see along the way. We imagine every detail, right down to the weather conditions and the clothes we'll wear. We busy ourselves with making reservations, shopping for clothes and supplies, getting our cars tuned up or our passports in order. We pack, unpack, and repack. We talk to our friends, travel agents, shop clerks, and anyone else who will listen and share in our excitement. People who have been where we're going offer their own experiences, insights, and advice. If stories crop up about problems or difficulties, we plan our own strategies for avoiding them. We don't imagine becoming tired, ill, or stranded. We envision perfection. Like the magazine photos of perfect plant specimens, the pictures we see and imagine of our vacation fill us with happy anticipation.

As I pore over my garden books and catalogs, drawings and lumber yard advertisements, I wonder about the idea of *just being* in relation to all of this research and *planning*. I ponder my relationship with my garden, my own place in the overall scheme of it. I examine the need for and my enjoyment of planning for the future while also *being here now*. I think about the Zen of this first stage of my gardening for the year.

Someone suggested to me that I simply throw some seeds around and see what happened; nature would take care of the rest. Someone else suggested tearing out all the existing wood, stone, brick, and plantings and allowing the space to grow completely wild. Still others thought my back garden would be a good place for a tennis or basketball court, a garage, or a large expanse of lawn. But none of these extremes appealed to me, or seemed right somehow. Surely some areas of nature left completely alone are necessary and good for the earth. And likewise, there is a place for purely human structures and spaces. But I wanted to work *with* nature in my garden, to become one with it; to be an integral, harmonious part *of* it. I wanted it to be better for my participation, as I wanted to benefit from its presence in my life.

The essence of Zen is simplicity, nonresistance, nonintervention, and awareness. It is mindfulness of everything's essential nature and being and acting in harmony with that. It is part of the essential nature of plant life to take root and grow. It is part of the essential nature of rock and stone to hold back water and soil runoff. It is part of the essential nature of humans to think, plan, learn, choose, design, and organize. Sometimes we carry this part of our essential nature too far, forgetting to be in harmony with all the other essential natures around us, but it's equally destructive to neglect our own essential nature and the positive contribution it can make to everything else. If we left plant life completely alone to fend for itself, we couldn't feed ourselves or the rest of the human population. But if we plan *consciously*, mindful of everything's essential nature, then all our thinking and planning can be of help to the rest of nature, providing a positive contribution to the planet.

Creativity is also a part of humanity's essential nature. But we don't create the materials that provide us with gardens; we create the idea of *garden* (just as we create the ideas of *vacation* or *journey*), and ultimately, the gardens themselves. This begins in our minds, early in the spring, with our seed catalogs, books, drawings, and plans. We envision our gardens into existence. We create, through the energy of our thoughts, the garden that will come into physical being later on. All the raw materials come from the earth, the rest comes from us.

We begin creating our garden by looking at what's already here: the sunshine and shade, the soil conditions and existing plant life. We can only grow a beautiful, abundant, and harmonious garden if we respect and honor its original nature. What *wants* to be here, what *likes* these conditions and will thrive here? It would be foolish to try to force a shade-loving plant to live in full, hot sunshine. It would be counterproductive to plant bush vegetables on a steep slope, where they'll have a hard time growing and we'll have a hard time tending them. The first step in planning our garden is to step back, be quiet, forget what *we* want for the moment, and just *look*. This is where the true beginning of the garden lies.

When we have learned what the space has to tell us, we can begin our research into working harmoniously with that. We can begin thinking of ourselves as part of nature's overall design, rather than conquerors, preparing to do battle with weeds, aphids, and clay soil. Our role is to blend into the garden, to become one with it, not to overcome it. What can we bring to this existing arrangement of nature to enhance it? How can we help the plant life get what it needs to flourish? How can we bring out the best in what we have to work with? What new elements can we bring in to harmonize with and improve this particular community of earth, air, water, and plant life? When we see ourselves as part of this community, all of our study, research, and planning enables us to make our best possible contribution to the garden.

It's like raising children. We can't *make* them into whatever we want them to be. All we can do is try to nurture and nourish the best that is already in them, their own essential natures. We can be a part of their lives that helps them, protects them, encourages them, and provides them with the conditions that will enable them to grow in their own way at their own pace. We can open our eyes to who they are and to what they need from us. Before they arrive, we anticipate, plan, and prepare. We educate ourselves on how to participate in their care and fill their needs. We draft a flexible plan for assisting their best possible development. And by putting who they are and what they need first, we are rewarded with far more than we could ever have imagined receiving back from them. The raw materials they are born with blossom into an abundance of beauty and love.

The raw materials of my own garden are fairly complex, since my property has been previously landscaped. It contains a variety of sunshine and shade, flowering plants and lawn, trees that have spread large roots throughout the earth, and a fence, deck, and patio arrangement complete with built-in planters. I also have a large dog (and doghouse) to consider in planning my backyard space. The front, side, and back of my property are each very different spaces, with very different conditions and uses. These differences need to be honored, while at the same time, the separate areas need to flow harmoniously into one another.

I begin with a drawing rendered by the landscaper hired by the previous owners. I can see that some changes were made to these plans: a child's sandbox moved from the patio area to a back corner of the lot; a tree left out to provide more sunshine at the center of the backyard. None of our plans are carved in stone. They evolve as we work to bring them into reality, changing to accommodate new information and solve unforeseen problems. They are alive, and like all living things, they grow over time.

My own plans begin with little additions and changes to the existing scheme; a few new perennials and bushes, a raised-bed vegetable garden in the sunniest part of the current perennial patch. I leave all the fences and wooden borders as they are, limiting my ideas to conform to their seniority here. But eventually, problems reveal themselves: How will I keep my dog out of the garden without tying her on a chain? How will I build my raised beds around or over the large oak roots bulging out of the ground? I try to *just look* at the spaces, to let them tell me what to do. And it works. My mind gradually breaks free of its adherence to the previous owners' plans. *Why not?* becomes my new mantra. *Why not* make use of all this sunshine in the middle of the yard by tearing out an area of lawn and putting my raised beds here? *Why not* move these smaller pines to the back fence area, away from the prime garden space? *Why not* build an arbor and cover it with climbing roses, even though everyone says roses are so hard to grow? *Why not*?

And so my plans blossom. An extension of the existing fence separating the deck and patio area from the garden area solves the dog problem. A gate off the deck allows for people and wheelbarrows to move back and forth freely. Current flower beds are stretched in size, while maintaining the integrity of shape. Raised beds spring up in the middle of the lawn, while low-lying perennials are allowed to creep and climb over the oak roots. Old and new ideas blend together and the garden evolves gracefully into its new form, honoring both.

Plans are drawn up, lists are made. Lumber yards, home improvement stores, and garden centers are visited—not for the purpose of buying anything yet, but just for looking, pricing, and nourishing ideas. Gradually, I become familiar with the varieties of plants that might do well here or there: which ones grow tall and which hug the ground; which ones keep to themselves and which spread throughout the garden like wildfire. Like new friends, I learn their names, characteristics, needs and desires, likes and dislikes. I cherish the visions my mind creates of the garden to come; relish the planning and plotting, the evolving picture at each stage of its development.

Perhaps the pleasure I get from all of this is nature's way of encouraging me to make my contribution to the earth on my small plot of land. Perhaps we love dreaming about, planning, studying, and designing our gardens because they need us to do it. Perhaps by doing what we love, we can enable them to do what they love: growing, flourishing, blossoming, and bearing fruit. Working together, we fulfill our higher purposes, our essential natures. The early days of planning our garden provide only a small sample of the pleasures to come. This is just the beginning of our garden journey.

SPRING

It was then the month of March, the days were growing longer, winter was departing, winter always carries with it something of our sadness; then April came, that daybreak of summer, fresh like every dawn, gay like every childhood; weeping a little sometimes like the infant that it is. Nature in this month has charming gleams which pass from the sky, the clouds, the trees, the fields, and the flowers, into the heart of man.

—Victor Hugo

In green underwood and cover Blossom by blossom Spring begins.

—A. C. Swinburne

Proud-pied April, dressed in all his trim, Hath put a spirit of youth in everything.

—William Shakespeare

The seasons cannot be hurried.
Spring comes, and the grass grows by itself.
                                        —Jon Kabat-Zinn

One morning, Babar, the king of the elephants, opens
his window. It's a sunny day in Celesteville. The
birds are chirping. The leaves and flowers seem to
have opened overnight. Babar is happy. "It's Spring!"
he shouts. "It's Spring!"
                                        —Laurent de Brunhoff

It's a late spring this year. Everyone says so. Things are taking their time coming up out of the ground, returning from their long winter slumber. The rhododendrons have finally burst into a blaze of bright purple blossoms. A few daffodils and tulips are timidly beginning to bloom.

I like the long spring. It gives me plenty of time to make the transition from the cold, dark, snowy winter to the bright warmth of summertime. It allows me to imagine, prepare for, and plan my garden. I'm not worried about all those lazy perennials, still snoozing beneath the soil or just now beginning to push tiny green stubs up from the ground. Other people shake their heads and wonder aloud if this or that will come back this year, whether they should begin thinking about planting something else in its place. I trust them to return . . . whenever they're ready.

The trees are suddenly full of small green buds, arriving as if from nowhere. Every place I look, the outlines of gray, skeletal tree forms are dotted with these infant leaves. They are beginning to soften the stark, barren branches and fill the air with a light green lace against the pale blue sky. The earth is waking up.

Spring has been the metaphor of poets since the beginning of time. It symbolizes hope, rebirth, fresh starts, new beginnings, purity, optimism, and youth. It feels like another chance, a clean slate. The days grow longer, and we have everything to look forward to. The rain washes away winter's debris and drabness and joins the sun in splashing everything with a bright green paintbrush. Gradually, other hues seep into the landscape, until the whole scene becomes a riotous blend of brilliant summer color.

But we are not there yet. Spring is its own season, its own special time. The time of birth and infancy, of slowly becoming aware of the earth's shifting mood. I walk outside and notice that my skin no longer tightens to brace itself against the cold air. *Mildness* is the perfect word for the air now. It does not assault me with either cold or heat. I move freely in and outdoors without a perceptible change in sensation. The air outdoors flows through my open windows, freshening the staleness inside without changing the temperature. The lilacs suddenly appear all over the neighborhood, announcing themselves with a burst of purple and white flowers, scented as nothing else in the world. We breathe in their lovely scent, rejoining the earth outdoors without the armor of heavy clothes and coats.

How can anyone not feel the joy of spring? How can we miss this amazing gift of renewal and reunion with the earth? How can we pass through this season oblivious to its glorious song? But we often do. Busy with work, families, and all the distractions of daily life, we allow spring to fly by us unnoticed. We let it pass without accepting its gifts, which are so often exactly what we need: a moment to breathe in the fresh air, a touch of nature's beauty and softness and comfort, a reminder that whatever happens, spring *will* come again— one thing in this world on which we can always rely.

I realize that I perform certain rituals in the spring: walks through my garden, the park, around the lakes. I wonder if I do this to reassure myself that once again, spring has not let me down. It is all here: trees and bushes all over the city are bursting with leaves, in all shades of green and even red and brown, some showing off with blossoms in pink or white or purple; the sweet scent of grass and earth and water fills the air and my lungs and my heart; even the slightly fishy smell of the lake stirs something in me that feels almost like *love*. The lake is beginning to fill with newly built docks and small sailboats claiming their designated homes for the season. All around the shoreline, hundreds of geese and their furry little families eat and swim and squawk, as crowded as the beaches will be with human families later in the season. *Ah yes, I remember this*, something in me says. *It's spring.*

Spring returns like clockwork, year after year, bringing with it a reminder of our true essential nature, our oneness with the planet, the stars, sun, moon, soil, rock, and earth. Along with the budding leaves and flowers, something in us opens up, lets down its guard, and bursts forth. The sun stays longer and fills our minds, hearts, and bodies with more light and more life. This effect is so well known that even the scientific community recognizes it, going so far as to name a disorder for the human response to winter's stingy daylight: Seasonal

Affective Disorder, or simply, Light Deprivation. Spring is nature's remedy.

As I turn my attention to my garden, I am filled with gratitude for this moment in the year when all is fresh and new. It is truly like being young again, like having nothing but possibilities before me. Never again in the season will there be so many choices to make, activities to begin, births to witness. It is the same feeling we get when we start any new project: school, marriage, jobs, relationships, or moving to a new place. I feel as though I'm in the pregnancy phase of this life cycle: planting, planning, laying the groundwork for a healthy, happy, abundant life to come.

Each individual seedling is its own life, and yet all the garden together is also one. Like people; like families; like humanity. Its awakening is individual as well as collective. Spring affects everything in the garden: earth, plants, animals, and birds—and the gardener. In spring we give ourselves another chance. We begin again, filled with new thoughts, plans, and enthusiasm. Old mistakes have faded from our memory, replaced by lessons learned. This time we'll do better. This year's garden will be the best ever. This season we'll take the time, relax and enjoy, and produce the biggest, most beautiful garden in the world! Whatever the summer brings, there is this moment in the spring when that glorious, perfect garden (and self) exists in our minds and hearts. And we set about beginning to make that image a reality.

There are so many aspects to spring that contribute to the joyous feelings it brings us. Freedom from snow and cold air, from gray skies and landscapes; extended periods of sunlight; the sense of clean slates and fresh starts. It is a time when we can hardly help but experience a heightened sense of awareness of everything around and inside us. This can actually be frightening if we're not accustomed to such awareness. We can try to withdraw from nature's cry to come out and face the sunlight. The earth awakens and calls us to join it.

On the surface, an awakened life may seem to be much more difficult than a more ordinary, sleepwalking kind of existence. It may be tempting to live out our days in air-conditioned, Musaked, cruise-controlled safety. In spring, nature confronts us with reality. *The earth is alive*! she screams. *And so are you*! Frightening, maybe, but incomparably joyous as well. What could be better than to feel really, truly, fully, totally alive! Awareness only frightens us because it's *different*. We're accustomed to a nice, safe level of sights, sounds, textures, feelings, and experiences. We've spent all winter trying to stay warm and dry and well fed despite nature's inhospitable conditions. Now she calls us to witness and experience something different: birth, growth, death, *life*. It stirs something primal in us, and our natural desire to rush right into it is often mixed with apprehension and fear. Fear of appearing foolish or childish (when was the last time you ran through a spring field holding onto the string of a kite?); fear of making a mistake (do you worry about gardening correctly or well enough?); fear of our own true natures (do you believe, on some level, that if you scratch the surface of a civilized human being you'll find only evil?).

To be fully here with spring is to let down our guard, to open up our hearts and minds like children, to really feel what it means to be alive. To *be here now*, completely and totally. Whether we answer it or not, come spring, we all hear the call. It sings in our ears, our minds, our emotions, relationships, work, and every aspect of our lives. Try as we might, we can't escape it. And if we stop trying to escape, if we let go and become one with the awakening earth, something happens to us. We wake up. We hear the birds chirp and see the grass grow and the leaves appear. We notice the squirrels and chipmunks scurrying about, looking for food or just playing with one another. We feel the longings of our own human heart, connected with all other human hearts, the desires for love and peace and joy, the natural tendency toward compassion and beauty. Once again, this year, our true essential nature is knocking at the door, ringing the alarm, sending us a wake-up call. The only question is, *are we listening?*

THE LILACS

Apparently Nature has a sense of humor, as well as considerable doubts about our perceptiveness; she gives a few clues to nudge us.

—Dorothy Gilman

"Even the grubby jobs, I find enjoyable."
"Oh, yeah? Like removing that tree stump, you mean?"
"Yes . . . well, I admit it was hard work. But there was a savage, primeval sort of joy in it."
"You chucked the pickaxe at the goat."
—Tom and Barbara Good (from *Good Neighbors*)

Gardening sometimes seems like a battle of wills between us and Mother Nature. Guess who wins? Not us, in all our knowledgeable, resourceful, powerful glory. It was actually Mother's Day when Mother Nature taught me this lesson.

There was a sort of gap in the middle of the garden along my back fence. On either side, tall trees balanced out the scene, but in the center (where something taller must have grown once, since there was a stump there when we moved in) there was a sort of lull, an expanse of low-lying foliage just crying out for something to reach up and fill the emptiness. I thought about some sort of evergreens and of various flowering bushes. I considered a bench covered by an arbor of climbing roses or morning glories, but it was too shady there, thanks to the canopy of tree limbs.

The decision was finally made to plant lilacs there; two or three lilac bushes, in fact, to fill and balance the space. Lilacs were chosen for their incomparable spring blossoms. At our last house, we were fortunate enough to have had a long row of large, old lilacs along the side of our driveway. They were actually rooted on our neighbor's property, but they reached over our driveway, loaded down with purple blossoms that filled our entire backyard with their lovely scent. Our neighbor kept apologizing for the lilacs, promising to cut them back. But we enthusiastically protested this idea, insisting that we loved the lilacs and enjoyed their return every spring. He told us to feel free to cut them, and we occasionally did, bringing the joy of their flowers into our home. Then, one beautiful spring day, we returned home from a day of work to find those lovely lilacs hacked nearly to nothing. It was one of the ugliest sights I have ever seen, causing a pain in my chest and a lump in my throat. Our neighbor came around, proudly asking if we'd seen his handiwork. What could we say? It was his property. Ever since then, we'd been determined to plant our own lilacs one day.

So we bought three healthy-looking bushes, one already showing signs of blossoms to come. We chose three spots in the garden where we thought they'd fill in nicely. My husband had been afraid they'd get too large and unruly (a fear based on his memories of a huge overgrown specimen in front of his parents' summer home) and had wanted to buy the dwarf variety. But I didn't want to limit what might develop in my unfolding garden and assured him that we could prune them annually if we wanted to and keep them as large or as small as we wished. I was a little concerned because the area where we wanted to put the lilacs was rather shady, and I'd heard that lilacs liked full sun. But I'd also been told that they would be all right in partial shade, they just wouldn't bloom as much.

The first place we dug was closest to the giant old oak tree that stands majestically over our backyard. The digging was hard, and I quickly deferred to my husband's superior strength of muscle. While he worked, I went about other garden chores, occasionally looking over to see how it was coming along. "There are a lot of roots in here," he grunted once, wiping the sweat dripping from his brow. He went to the garage to get different tools. I went back to my Johnny-jump-ups.

After a while, I just stood watching the unfolding drama of my dear husband versus Mother Nature. He began angrily hacking away at the roots with an ax. When I saw large splinters of wood coming out of the ground, I finally walked over to where he was working. "Don't you think it's time to give that up?" I said, as quietly and calmly as I possibly could. He threw the ax down on the ground and fell into a sitting position. He wiped the sweat from his face, which had that "*Now* she tells me!" look on it. After a moment, he said, "I think I can get it in there," not wanting to give up now, with so much pain invested in the project. "But even if you do," I answered softly, "how will its roots get nourishment or have room to grow?" Resignedly, he threw down the towel he was using to dry his face and neck. "Yeah, you're right," he conceded.

He filled up the small hole he had managed to produce and proceeded to the other two spots we had chosen, farther away from the oak tree. A couple of good stabs with the spade told us these spots would be no better than the first. "Well, back to the drawing board," he sighed. We walked around the garden, consulted our drawings and plans, and discussed various possibilities. There was one edge of the lawn where we'd planned to plant nothing, but just to allow the grass to grow all the way to the fence. The rest of the yard had plantings, trees, and bushes all around the outer edge. This was the spot we'd thought we'd leave alone, maybe place a couple of chairs or a bench and possibly even that arbor covered with climbing roses over it—if we got around to it this year. But it seemed to be the only reasonable place to put the lilacs except for the edge of the patio, where I'd planned to plant my herb garden. It was far enough away from that monstrous oak to dig up the ground and for the lilacs to spread out some roots of their own. It was also much sunnier than our original plan.

We decided to leave the herb garden plans alone and dug out the sod in a strip from one existing border to another. We turned over the soil, added peat moss and fresh topsoil, and edged it with black plastic (recycled, of course) lawn edging. We planted the lilac bushes there in a row.

Suddenly, the backyard had a pleasing, finished look about it. The garden had literally come full circle. It was as if this missing piece of the puzzle had suddenly been fit into place. We had listened, albeit somewhat unwillingly, to what Mother Nature was telling us to do and the lilacs clearly ended up where they had belonged all along. They quickly took to the sunny spot, growing, flourishing, and blessing us with heaven-scented blossoms almost immediately. We can hardly imagine them anywhere else or remember what the spot looked like without them. It's as if they'd always been there.

Mother Nature, like all good, loving mothers, nudges us in the right direction for our own and ultimately the highest good. But she can only do that when we hush and listen. The professional landscapers, who had been paid handsomely by the previous owners to design and plant our property, had apparently not taken this into consideration once their plan was set. No less than three small trees had died and been removed soon after their planting. We'd had to remove one of them ourselves after moving in. It had been set into a hole barely big enough for its tender roots, surrounded by a network of oak roots so strong that it took an ax (and stronger muscles than mine) to break them. The landscapers had battled Mother Nature and, determined to win, had killed an innocent tree—*three* innocent trees.

Mother Nature doesn't tell us what to do. She shows us *what is*. We can learn to go along with that, or we can fight it and ultimately destroy it. Those are the only two choices there are, because *what is* isn't going to change just because we want it to. And that's a very good thing; Mother Nature has things well in hand. Sometimes the only way for us to win is to give up and let her win. She will anyway. Why make it hard on ourselves?

We probably could have managed to dig three holes near that oak tree large enough to stick those lilac bushes in the ground. But what would have happened? What would those poor bushes have looked like today? What would we have felt like today, looking at them, digging up their remains and throwing them on the compost heap? What would we have done with that empty space by the fence, the broken circle? How would we have felt about that? From now on, whenever I think I know what's best in a battle with Nature, I remember the lilacs—and listen.

THE RAISED BEDS

*If you can meet with Triumph and Disaster
And treat those two imposters just the same.*
                                        —Rudyard Kipling

*Great events make me quiet and calm; it is only
trifles that irritate my nerves.*
                                        —Queen Victoria

There is no joy but calm!
                                        —Alfred, Lord Tennyson

I had spent days and days on the raised beds, digging out sod, building the wooden frames, cutting out tree roots, filling in the cleared spaces with compost, peat moss, and topsoil. Finally, I'd bought seeds and seedlings to plant. I'd carefully planned where everything should go, based on sunlight, companion planting, and length of maturity. I had put in eight pepper plants, sixteen tomato plants (each with its own basil seedling right next to it, the way my grandmother had always done), a row of leeks, and four eggplant, six cucumber, and six zucchini plants. I'd put in rows of lettuce, green bean, and carrot seeds, along with plenty of onion sets.

Outside my raised beds, I had perennials, lilac bushes, and an herb garden, freshly planted with a variety of small plants—except for the mint, of course, which had to be confined to its own built-in planter on the deck, due to its tendency to spread like wildfire and take over the entire garden.

The very morning after I'd done all this planting, there was a torrential rainstorm. Early in the morning, I heard the heavy rainfall on my roof, and all I could think was, *Oh no, my garden is ruined.* When the rain subsided, I could see that my two raised beds had been transformed into two pools of well-confined water. As time went by, it became clear that the water was not going to soak in or drain off. A great deal of my garden was, in fact, ruined. What had I done wrong? What should I have done that I hadn't? Filled them up with more soil so that there would be no room for all that water? Bored holes into the wooden frames to let the excess water drain away? Or, easiest of all, simply planted the garden in the cleared-off spaces without the wood frames at all? Nothing else in the garden was flooded or ruined. The herbs, while knocked about a bit by the force of the downpour, were popping back up, refreshed and nourished by the deluge. The perennials glowed from the cleansing shower they'd received. Even the little potted plants I was baby-sitting for a friend who was moving looked fine. It was just those raised beds. I had clearly made some *big* mistake there.

There was a time in my life when I know this would have done me in. A few short years ago, I would have been crying, swearing, and running outdoors in the rain trying to bail out the water, to save the plants and seeds I had worked so hard to get into the ground. I would have been embarrassed and ashamed to face my neighbor, whom I had caught silently peeking over the fence the day before to see what I was doing. I would have felt this failure, this attack on my work, in the pit of my stomach for days. But now I simply sat at my kitchen table, looking out the window, thinking of what I might do next and already planning the new plants and seeds I would have to buy. I calmly tied up my hair, poured another cup of coffee, found my garden gloves, and headed outside.

The clouds had broken; the sky was light. Not really knowing what I might do, if anything, I went to survey the damage (like a president visiting the scene of some natural disaster). My first impression was that it was not nearly as bad as it had looked from the window, as bad as I had feared. That water was making some feeble attempt to drain off as best it could. Without really thinking or deciding to do it, I reached down and tried to lift the wooden frame a bit. It came up easily, and as I held it there, and inch or less off the ground, the pool of water quickly drained away into the surrounding lawn. I did the same thing with the other wood frame. Noticing certain pools that had formed due to indentations in the soil, I traced little trenches in paths from the pools to the edge where the water drained away. Then I placed a few flattish stones under the wood frame at the spots where I'd drained off the water. It continued to flow there under the frame and away into the lawn.

I noticed that the plants looked remarkably well. I needn't buy any new tomatoes, peppers, basil, eggplant, cucumbers, zucchini, leeks, or onion sets. Only one tomato plant needed to be straightened up and the soil firmed around it. The seeds, rather than being washed away wholesale, had simply settled into the soggy soil where they were. A few beans had floated to the surface, and I simply pushed them back under the soil. Rather than starting over, I would wait to see what came up and where. I hadn't used up all my seeds and still had plenty to plant later. So what if the rows weren't perfectly straight anymore? All was well.

A solid week of rain has finally ended, and I'm thinking now about how to provide better drainage for my raised beds. Perhaps when it's dryer outdoors, I'll bore some holes in the wooden frames. Or maybe I'll loosen the joints where the boards are screwed together and let the water drain out between them. Or maybe I'll lift them out, dig a trench, and put them back deeper than before, allowing the water to drain off the top of the soil. I've found a book that says you should put four inches of rock in your raised bed before you put in the compost, peat, and topsoil. A little too late for that! But it also suggests drilling "weep holes" in the wood frame, so that's what I'll do.

How fortunate that this deluge happened right at the beginning of the season so that I could learn about this drainage problem and do something about it. *Things happen so that we can learn from them*—a simple fact of life, but one that seems to take us so long and so much trouble to learn. If I had been upset, would I have seen the simple thing to do? If I'd cried and sworn and felt attacked, would anything have changed? I went out there ready to apologize to my seeds and plants for my mistakes, my failure. Instead, I found them dealing with the situation, ready and willing to recover. I don't even know what made me lift up the wooden frame. Impulse? Reflex? Garden fairies whispering in my ear? I do know that I had not expected it to lift up so easily or to be able to resolve the problem so quickly and inexpensively. How many things in life might work if only we'd try them, if only we'd let go of thinking so much about whether or not we believe they will work? We want guarantees. We don't want to experiment with an open mind and heart. We want to reason everything out, plot it and plan it and make it work on paper, and then we'll try it (maybe). That method could have been applied here, possibly with exactly the same results. But that's not what happened. I simply let go and did whatever came naturally.

Instinct? Intuition? My true essential nature as part of the garden, rather than its owner or master? The garden has recovered from the crashing floodwaters, and so have I. It's all been a pleasant, even a wonderful experience. Perhaps now the garden knows that it can trust me to help it, to give it what it needs, rather than what I want to think it needs. To let it tell me what to do. To work in harmony with it. How differently this whole event might have been if I'd gotten (reasonably and logically) upset.

I now trust my garden to cope with less-than-perfect conditions. And yet, perhaps nature is always perfect—*we're* the ones who respond to it with all of our fear, anger, worry, and doubt. Perhaps this torrent of rain was the perfect thing to happen—for my garden and for me. The garden seems to be no worse for wear. In fact, my plants are growing by leaps and bounds, their roots happily drinking up a nearly endless supply of nourishment from the drenched soil. And I am a little more confident that together, my garden and I can deal with anything that happens. I am more likely to remember that *a little calmness goes a long way*, in the garden and everywhere else.

WORK

*A red tulip suddenly appeared in my garden,
followed by a purple one. And suddenly it was April,
and the sound of pinkwinks could be heard from the
bogs at night. It was time to start planting.*
—Dorothy Gilman

*Non-doing can arise within action as well as stillness.
The inward stillness of the doer merges with the
outward activity to such an extent that the action
does itself.*
—Jon Kabat-Zinn

*What a man needs in gardening is a cast-iron back
with a hinge on it.*
—Charles Dudley Warner

There is a period in the spring when a gardener's life is one of
frenzied activity and endless work. After all the research and planning,
the deciding and imagining, comes the time to *act*. Decisions become
shopping lists; ideas become to-do lists. Between the quiet dormancy

of winter and the casual maintenance of summer is sandwiched a brief flurry of intense activity. As Barbara Good, a character in a 1970s British television comedy about a self-sufficient suburban couple once put it, "That Mother Nature woman! She has a holiday all winter long, and then comes back in the spring, and BANG! WALLOP! Goes raving mad!"

There is an enormous amount of work to be done in the garden early in the season. After a while, the plants grow on their own, and aside from the regular watering, weeding, and harvesting, the garden pretty much tends itself. But in the beginning, there is an awful lot of *doing* to gardening. While on the surface, the concept of *doing* seems to be opposed to the whole idea of Zen, the physical labor that is required in the beginning of gardening presents us with a perfect opportunity to practice. It is a matter of how we do what we do.

Being totally immersed in an activity makes it a Zen experience. When you're in this state, time stands still; nothing else in the world exists for you. The past and the future find no place in your mind, which is completely absorbed in the present moment. You and the action you are performing become one, until you *are* the action, not a body doing it.

All the hard work required in the beginning of creating a garden provides a perfect opportunity for this kind of experience. We can lose ourselves in the work, melt into it, become one with it. Pure physical labor and repetitive tasks lend themselves easily to the letting go of our egos and the constant chatter usually present on our minds. We are carried along with the flow of energy, an inseparable part of it. Digging, weeding, and planting, we are as close to our original nature as we ever are, like the bees and ants around us, performing our work intuitively, unthinkingly, and mindfully.

How can we be unthinking and mindful at the same time? Because mindfulness means letting go of thinking, deciding, reasoning, labeling, and judging. We *just do*. Our whole being becomes the action we are doing, and there is no division or separation between the doer and the action. We forget ourselves for a time and allow ourselves to be part of something else—the energy of the universe and the action that flows naturally from it. It comes in the moment after all the planning, deciding, choosing, and getting ready for our work. It comes in the moment before the work is done and we shift into the mode of standing back to see what's been done. It is in the magical moment when nothing else exists except the task itself.

The fourth of July came on a Tuesday this year. The long weekend provided a perfect opportunity for gardening. On Saturday the weather was warm but not hot, and overcast, but not rainy. Perfect gardening weather. I set about digging, weeding, and planting early in the morning. The hours slipped by unnoticed. Before I knew it, it was late afternoon. I hadn't stopped for food or anything else. I was totally immersed in my gardening.

My body reached and stretched, pulled, pushed, and lifted. I lifted from my legs rather than my back, as experts are always reminding us to do in order to avoid back injuries. My muscles responded to my every command to push them just a little bit further, to work just a little bit harder and longer. By the end of the day, they ached and I felt great. The next morning I awoke a little stiff and achy, but stretched a little to warm up before another day in the garden. I believed that if I just kept at it, my muscles would continue to perform and if I stopped suddenly, they would really get stiff and sore. I took an aspirin substitute and soldiered on. I didn't give in to the aches, and worked another two full days digging, bending, kneeling, squatting, sitting on the ground, moving irises, planting daylilies, phlox, bleeding hearts, heather, and veronica. I dealt with problems in my vegetable patch, adding petunias, anise, garlic, and more marigolds, onions, and basil in an effort to ward off what seemed to be an aphid-borne mosaic blight appearing on my pepper plants.

After three long days of labor, my garden was pretty well set for the season. I felt satisfied and triumphant. The aches in the backs of my legs felt like battle scars, war wounds of which I could be proud. *No pain, no gain*, right? The tiredness I felt seemed well earned and I looked forward to a holiday of barbecues and fireworks.

But on the morning of the Fourth, I woke up to extremely sore muscles. The backs of my legs felt like two-ton weights, swollen and screaming with pain. I could barely walk. No position was more comfortable than another, no movement possible without tremendous effort and misery. I gulped down painkillers and tried to remember whether heat or ice was the appropriate treatment for whatever I had done to myself. I finally decided on ice, because of the swelling, and spent most of the holiday miserably immobile with ice packs under my legs.

It was a stormy day, and while I managed to grill vegetables outdoors between rain showers, many of the planned fireworks displays were canceled. My Fourth of July went off with a fizzle rather than a bang. But when you're in a lot of pain, it's hard to think about anything else. I wondered why my leg muscles hadn't performed as I'd expected. At what point had they given out, had I pushed them too far? What messages had I missed to stop and take a break, to drink a glass of water or eat a meal or take a nap? When had I slipped out of my Zen attitude of flowing with the energy of Nature and into the old domineering, conquering one? What decisions had I made about how it was going to be instead of letting myself be told? When had I stopped being the action performed and resumed my arrogant human position as the one performing the action?

Gardening is hard work. Muscles do get taxed. But pushing one-self over the edge is not natural, it's nonsense. And it's self-defeating. And it's not Zen. I had stopped listening to the soft voice of Nature whispering in my ear, and instead followed the cheerleader of my ego: *Get one more thing done; It's too early for a break; If you just keep going, you can finish it all today.* Without realizing it, I had passed the point of being lost in my work and gone over the line into the ego zone. I had lost the Zen of my gardening experience for that weekend.

It happens often, this one-step-beyond syndrome. My husband does yard work until a muscle pain tells him to stop; my neighbor paints his house until his weak knees give out, finally requiring surgery. We work until we have rendered ourselves unfit to do that or anything else. And we're proud of it. Something in our human ego tells us that this is a good thing to do. But what's good about it? I spent a week in pain and misery, hardly able to walk, unable to move normally for even longer. My husband pulled a muscle under his arm, causing him pain and days of inactivity. My neighbor lost almost a whole summer of yard work and house-painting jobs due to his knee surgery. I suspect we all could have gained more without the pain.

Work is a wonderful thing. It gives us the present moment joy of nonaction within action and the pleasure of accomplishment afterward. As the season wears on and I loll through the more sedate stages of my garden's evolution for this year, I will remember the busy period, filled with all that frenzied work, and wish I had enjoyed it more, in Zen mindfulness.

THE OAK TREE

If you understand, things are as they are.
If you do not understand, things are as they are.
— Zen verse

Life never stands still.
If I had known this, I might have had more faith.
— Dorothy Gilman

    Nearly every area of my life was troubled. I had held on with hope and faith for months, but everything had only gotten worse and worse. None of the things I'd wanted, prayed for, and visualized had happened. People I'd trusted had lied to me and stolen my work, a writer's only real property. And it happened at a time when I could least afford the financial burden it cost me. Everything seemed to be crashing to a crisis point at once. I felt abandoned and despairing. After all these years of life, I am still shocked when outright deceit is revealed—as it always is, eventually. I continue to be startled by the harm people do to one another. And the feelings that are stirred within me by these events upset me as much as the events themselves.

    Living Zen doesn't mean that nothing will ever again happen to or around you. People will continue doing things that you would never do to them or anyone else. Accidents, earthquakes, and bombings will forever pepper our lives with anguish and sorrow. Cruelty and ignorance will continue to plague us. The only question is, *How will we respond to them*? The things that were happening in my life filled me with anger—even rage—and deep sorrow. I struggled with self-doubt and agonized over how I could have possibly brought these events on myself. I felt hostile and wounded at the same time. And I hated feeling all of that.

Thoughts of every possible reaction from lawsuits to angry letters cut through my mind like a jagged-edged knife, destroying my peace. At the same time, my mind echoed with old, forgotten platitudes such as, "Success is the best revenge." But the word *revenge* hurt my sensibilities as much as the anger and sadness. I didn't want revenge; I didn't want to make anyone pay for their deception and the harm they had done to me. I didn't want to feel hurt, angry, or vengeful. On the other hand, I had truly been victimized. There was another unacceptable word; I would not become a *victim*. Should I turn the other cheek? Should I do nothing?

In the midst of all this, I decided to throw the I Ching, to see if I could glean some wisdom from the ancient Chinese oracle. I threw the three coins six times and came up with the twenty-eighth hexagram, *Greatness in Excess* or *Preponderance of the Great*. I read two different translation/interpretation books and both said that many important areas of conflict in my life were coming to a head all at once and there was nothing I could do to stop or hold them off any longer. The oracle advised me to stand like a strong tree while the floodwaters crashed all around me; that soon they would subside because it is water's nature to seek its own level. I should remain calm and steadfast through the storm, and I would come out of it all right.

I thought a lot about that image of the strong tree withstanding the floodwaters. In my backyard there stands a giant oak tree. It has been there for perhaps one hundred years. It has withstood that many frigid, snowy winters, hot summers, fierce thunderstorms, and gentle rains. It has stood straight and tall while everything around it evolved from open prairie to bustling city. It has withstood its branches being amputated to make way for electrical and telephone wires and the ground around it being covered with concrete. It has calmly allowed children and squirrels to play all over it and birds to make their homes in its branches.

This huge oak tree has remained essentially the same through all the changes surrounding it. It is tall and strong and straight and healthy. It does not bend or break, at least not under any force it has so far encountered in its one hundred years. It is itself—strong, solid, and true—through whatever happens. It feels no anger or emotion, no sorrow or anguish. It has no ego, and yet it withstands all manner of attack. It serves its essential nature, its true spirit.

Things did not get better immediately after I threw that I Ching message. In fact, even more areas of my life that I had thought were perfectly fine and peaceful suddenly erupted with new problems. I kept thinking, through it all, of that oak tree in my backyard, standing tall and straight and strong and calm while floodwaters splashed and lightning crackled all around it. This vision helped me to remain calm and peaceful while several serious problems culminated in my life. I learned the difference between stubbornly trying to force things and people to be the way I wanted them to be on the one-hand, and simply remaining firm in myself, in my true nature and essential being, and trusting in the essential nature of the universe on the other.

As I saw myself standing calmly like the oak through this stormy time, I realized that I didn't have to fight against people and problems; I wasn't getting drawn into pointless arguments and manipulative games with other people or into fearful despairing reactions to events and circumstances. I stood peacefully, like that oak tree, while events unfolded around me. In time, some difficulties subsided, some problems worked themselves out, and some even seemed to evaporate because of my calmness in facing them. As it is the nature of water to seek its own level, it is the nature of problems to eventually be resolved, one way or another. It is the nature of pain and anger to subside. It is the nature of life for things to change. I went on to greater successes, not out of revenge, but simply by following the correct path of my true peaceful nature.

In Zen, we do not *react*, we *respond* with the calm, peaceful strength of the giant oak. It is still true that I was lied to and stolen from. That is a fact, but it is not a sentence to misery and pain. In fact, I am now grateful for the experience. It taught me the lesson of the oak tree, the strength that lies within peaceful acceptance of what is. It taught me to serve my spirit, not my ego. I am still shocked by deception. Cynicism has not won another victim. I have not changed my essential nature because of what others have done or things that have happened. I have discovered within myself the strength of the oak tree.

I look at the giant oak tree in my backyard more frequently now, and more closely. It holds great meaning for me and still gives me comfort and wisdom. I see the rope that hangs from its largest and strongest branch, a relic of some child's swing that hung there long ago. I see the tree's responsibility to the rope, the swing, the child, and the parents who entrusted their child to the tree's strength and reliability. I see the scars of wounds from the electric saw and the woodpecker's bill that have now healed over. I see the old dead, dry leaves, bark, and branches letting go easily with the wind and falling gracefully to the ground when the time is right. I see, too, the new growth: fresh infant buds and thin green branches stretching out and up toward the sun.

The oak tree, in doing all of this, is simply being an oak tree. It is being true to its essential nature. I, too, am being true to my essential nature when I am calm, peaceful, strong, and steadfast; when I am responsible and reliable; when I withstand life's wounds and go on to heal; when I let go gracefully of the old qualities, circumstances, and relationships that once were mine but are no longer right or good for me to hold onto; and when I allow new growth to continually stretch me in new directions, while I remain firmly rooted in my true essential nature. I am being true to my essential nature—my spirit— when I am surprised by the brutality of life's raging storms.

Someday, off in the distant future, that tree will fall or be cut down, just as my own life on this earth will eventually come to an end. But until then, I will follow the example of the giant oak. We will stand here in the sunshine and the rain, the warmth and gentleness of a summer's breeze and the frigid isolation of a winter's night.

We will stand straight and tall while the floodwaters crash and the lightning crackles all around us. We will be true to our essential natures and let all other things and people be true to theirs. We will *just be*—me and the mighty oak tree.

HERE COMES THE SUN

Summer afternoon—summer afternoon; to me those have always been the two most beautiful words in the English language.

—Edith Wharton

Can it be that there was only one summer when I was ten?

—May Swenson

*Summertime—
and the livin' is easy.*

—Ira Gershwin

When summer finally arrives, it brings with it more than warm weather. It brings memories, feelings, and metaphors. The scents of beach and city, ballpark and cornfield, barbecues and blossoms; the feel of sand and soil, sun and water, bare skin and sweat; the tastes of fresh green beans, crisp lettuce, juicy watermelon, and ice cream; the sights of green fields and bright flower beds. Summer. It's a season, a feeling, an attitude. If spring is nature's metaphor for rebirth or youth, them summer symbolizes the essence, the very spirit of freedom.

From the time we are babies, summer means freedom from being confined indoors, from school, from work, from home. It's vacation time, playtime, get-away-from-it-all time. It's time for lazing in a hammock, reading or sleeping; for splashing the heat away in a lake or pool; for running, biking, swimming, and playing ball. It's time for eating outdoors, in backyards, on beaches, park benches, or the terrace of a fine restaurant. It's time for lake cabins, canoes, fishing, and waterskiing. It's time for fireworks and open fire hydrants. It's time for gardens.

When I was a child, summer meant mornings of sleeping late and afternoons spent in the cool branches of the tree next to my house, with Nancy Drew mysteries and Popsicles. It meant riding bikes all around the neighborhood with friends, going nowhere in particular and stopping only for the Good Humor truck. It meant trying to fry eggs on sidewalks on the hottest days and running through rain showers in our swim suits. It meant catching fireflies in our hands and caterpillars in jars, hoping they'd turn into butterflies before our very eyes (they never did). Summer meant my grandmother's garden; the scent of tomato plants and basil and mint; popping the sweet peas that climbed the arbor over the bench my grandfather had built himself; eating fried pepper sandwiches and lemon Italian ice on a blanket in the backyard.

When I was older, summer meant the beach. Friends, parties, boys. Wet, sandy swimsuits and suntans and volleyball games and moonlit romance. We played cards on our towels and flirted with strangers. We read magazines and drank (sometimes spiked) sodas. We took our first jobs and drove our parents' cars for the first time. We did a lot of things for the first time. We were free. Free from adult supervision, school-night curfews, and dependence for transportation; free from studying and worrying about our grades and our futures; free from snow and cold and all those heavy clothes. We didn't go in much for gardening.

As an adult, summer began to lose some of its specialness for me. One quickly discovers that work, unlike school, goes on year round with only a week or two of freedom annually. Vacations require money, planning, packing, transportation, food, laundry, and endless arrangements. Summer becomes a day care problem for school-age children. The warmer weather brings with it fatigue, bugs, and sandy car seats. Freedom doesn't seem to enter into it.

But the magic of gardening reappeared in my life when I had a backyard and a family of my own. I rediscovered the joys of earth and flower and fruit. I watched my daughter delight in my garden as I had in my grandmother's. Every day after work, I could escape to my garden; every weekend I could revel in the earthy scent and texture of soil and stem, blossom and vegetation. In nature, I found my freedom again.

While I had been told that some people simply had a green thumb, while others did not, I found that gardening worked best when fretted about the least. I just did it. Impatiens in the shade, marigolds in the sun; tomato plants staked up against the fence, cucumbers climbing a lattice trellis; morning glories winding up the tall pole to the bird house and covering it like an ivy-covered cottage; broccoli, Brussels sprouts, carrots, beets, lettuce, beans, and peppers wherever there was room for them. Not everything was a smashing success, but so what? I was out to have fun, to explore and experiment, to enjoy the freedom from judgments and grades, from expectations and quests for perfection. I was free to just play in my little plot of earth.

I would not be the enthusiastic, loving (albeit far from expert) gardener that I am now if I had started out believing that I had to do things in a certain way and produce certain results, if I had forgotten that summertime is playtime. My garden is my playground, the place where I don't have to be perfect in any way. My flowers and vegetables and I play together, and the soil and grass and trees join in the fun. In the summer, they get to grow, creep, climb, flourish, flower, and bear fruit; they get sunshine, fresh warm air, rain, and me fussing over them. What could be more fun than that for a living thing that must lie sleeping beneath the cold ground the rest of the year? They aren't looking for human companions with green thumbs, just for people with a sense of fun and freedom to join them in their brief season of festivity. We are all on vacation together.

There is a Zen saying that when it is summer, everywhere is summer. The field and the city, the lake and the sidewalk, the air-conditioned office and the dark space under the hosta leaves in my backyard. Summer permeates the sky and the soil, the air in my lungs and the images in my eyes. Everywhere, it is impossible to escape the summer-ness of everything. It lives and breathes through us, around us, under our feet, and over our heads. Children climb trees and ride bikes and try frying eggs on sidewalks; teenagers laugh at the beach, in cars, and under the moon; old men blot their foreheads with handkerchiefs and play checkers in the park. All over town, round green tomatoes weigh down their vines, and the petunias are as red in front of the Capitol building as they are in vacant lots turned into community gardens. Everywhere is summer.

It is summer for our cats and dogs, for the birds, squirrels, chipmunks, rabbits, and raccoons that share our community. It is summer for the grass and dandelions, the coleus and marigolds, the oak and the sunflower. It is summer indoors and out; upstairs and down; on the beach and in the laundromat. Summer comes equally to the fish in the cool, dark lake and to the fisherman on the hot, sunny dock. It does not pick and choose. It just *is*, everywhere.

If summer comes the same whether I garden or not, I will garden. If summer comes the same whether or not I feel free, I will feel free. I will let summer into my bones, my cells, and my heart. I will think about the fall and winter when they come; I will be in summer all summer long. I will be mindful of summer this year, as I was as a child and a teenager. I will savor every day, every moment, every ray of sunshine and drop of warm rain. I will hear the birds and the woodpeckers and the wind chimes. I will smell the leaves and blossoms as well as the fumes from the city buses and the charbroiling steaks from the restaurant around the corner. Everywhere is summer, whether I am aware or not. I will be aware.

ST. FRANCIS OF ASSISI

Standeth God in the shadow, keeping watch above his own.

—James Russell Lowell

Someone once came upon Saint Francis hoeing in his garden, and asked him what he would do if he found out that the world would end the following day. Without a pause, Saint Francis replied, "I'd keep on hoeing."

—Abd al-Hayy Moore

I'll admit I've always been something of a snob when it comes to garden statuary. I could never see the value in punctuating a completely natural setting with concrete birdbaths or plastic deer. I never understood the desire for colorful garden gnomes and pink flamingos. Even the less obviously tacky Grecian urns and Roman cherubs seemed to me belonging strictly on huge estates with formal gardens. And even there, I wasn't crazy about them. I always thought that if I had that much money, I'd never clutter up my property with cheap imitations of Michaelangelo-type classics.

So I had never paid much attention to such wares in the garden stores and responded only with a condescending smirk when they were pointed out to me. Then one day I was stopped short by the sight of one in a department store. This was a higher-priced store, displaying better-quality products on its marble and floral-carpeted floors. As I headed quickly toward the fine china department to pick up a friend's bridal registry list, I passed a collection of garden pots, planters, and wrought-iron chairs. Mixed among these expensive items were stone statues in soft grays and greens, with dark antiquing shading their cracks and crevices. There were gargoyles, cherubs, angels, and a seated child reading a book. And there was a statue of St. Francis of Assisi. It stood about two feet high, carved (or molded, I suppose) out of some very heavy stone (probably concrete) in a muted, antiqued green.

I stopped and stared at it. There was nothing garish or cheap-looking about it. In fact, it was hauntingly beautiful. I couldn't take my eyes off it. I kept imagining it in my garden, half hidden among the greenery, in a corner under three rather small trees. Not as a shrine to the saint or an accent piece to brighten up the garden, but blending in with the leaves and flowers, the soil and shade, nearly invisible.

St. Francis of Assisi is the patron saint of nature and animals. He is always depicted with birds and woodland animals surrounding him, drawn to him. Legend has it that he was a wild, rich young man who had some sort of conversion experience after which he lived a simple, natural life, surrounded by birds and animals, who loved him. When my husband, who is a lover of math and computers, visited Italy as a student many years ago, he had what was (aside from the birth of our daughter) the only experience of his life that he calls "spiritual." Touring the village of Assisi, he entered the cloister of St. Francis and found himself overwhelmed by a sense of presence, of some other-worldly essence surrounding and rushing through him. As the other tourists filed through, he stopped, as if frozen to the spot. He couldn't leave. He didn't want to leave this profound peace and spirituality that had overtaken his senses. He described it as "chills" that ran up and down his spine, a feeling of almost being "in a trance." His fellow students laughed when he told them about it, but the locals just nod ded, grunting, "That's St. Francis," as if it were the most natural thing in the world.

I *had* to buy the statue of St. Francis for my garden. It was expensive, though I soothed my conscience with the fact that it was on sale. It was too heavy for me to deal with, so I had it sent to my home, since delivery was free. I dug out a little space between the perennials under the three trees, buried three coins in a little hole (for luck and prosperity), covered it up, and placed the statue over it. The surrounding foliage has grown taller now and nearly hides the statue completely.

Sometimes, in the garden, I talk to Frank—that's what I've taken to calling him—and I ask him to deal with the ground squirrels that have been eating my seedlings. I ask him what I did wrong with the phlox or whether I should move the catmint. He doesn't answer me, of course, but I don't think it hurts to talk to him. Maybe he *is* listening and putting the answers in front of me when I need them. There are those who say that gardens are full of fairies and angels, watching over the plants and helping them grow. The Findhorn Garden in Scotland is a well-known community where the biggest, healthiest vegetables imaginable are grown, thanks to a resident group of fairies, according to those who run the garden.

I don't know if there are fairies or angels living in my garden, but there *is* Frank. He is definitely there, a strong presence in stone and spirit. What he adds to my collection of leaves, flowers, fruits, vegetables, and herbs is much more than a stone representation of a man. It's a reminder of my husband's experience in Italy, of the love we need to have for other creatures and everything natural on this earth, and of our connectedness to it all. It makes me feel like a true friend to animals and plants; their sister, mother, protector, and child all at once. It makes me think of people I have seen standing calmly and happily, covered with bees. I wonder if I could ever have that kind of total trust and love with the other living beings of the earth.

I don't eat meat and I am kind to animals, but I know I still fear them on some level. Not the cats and dogs in my house, of course, but some other animals—and bees, especially. When I was a small child, my older sister persuaded me to stick my hand in a bush and I was promptly stung by a bee. I guess she was too afraid to do it herself, to see if the neighbor boy who had told her there were bees in there was telling the truth. I'd hate to think that she did it on purpose. Anyway, I'm not someone who could stand around covered with bees. And in a way, that makes me sad: that we're so out of touch with the other creatures with whom we share the planet. I'd like to be like St. Francis, but I don't know if I really want birds sitting on my shoulders.

I love the animals in my home, who are part of my family. I even love the ducks that nest in my front yard every spring and then disappear. I love the robins on my lawn, the butterflies on my flowers, the squirrels that run up and down the trees in my yard, and the chipmunk who sits on my deck every morning—but we keep our distance from one another. They have their space and I have mine. I wonder what happened to St. Francis to make him turn from a drunken reveler into a bird and bunny magnet.

Since I am not as perfect as he is in this area, I am glad to have Frank in my garden. I talk to him about the garden and about other things, too. He's a good listener. Maybe that's why animals love him: he just stands there quietly, calm and unthreatening, peaceful and silent. Maybe we bring too much of our noise and ego into the world and into the garden. Maybe we need to be a little more soft, gentle, and quiet and let the animals come to us. Maybe we need to be a little more humble out there in the natural world. Maybe that's what St. Francis learned; maybe he went from being a loud, boisterous big shot to being just one of the little creatures of the forest. And that's when he found his true power.

I'm not such a snob about garden decoration anymore. I figure everyone must have their reasons for putting little windmills and reflecting globes about their yards. Who knows what lessons these objects might teach them or experiences they might bring to mind? No one else looking at Frank under my trees could ever guess all that he means to me. So, when it comes to garden statuary, I've stopped smirking and judging. I accept whatever I see, wherever I see it. Everything is always perfect right where it is. Maybe it won't always be there, but when it is, that's where it belongs. In Zen, we learn that every moment is perfect as it is—even moments when pink flamingos and red-capped gnomes frolic on the lawn.

Only one thing bothers me a little about our St. Francis: his mouth is clearly frowning. I keep looking to see if maybe his face is just expressionless or pensive or prayerful or something, but I can't convince myself that the corners of his mouth don't turn decidedly downward. His face is more than just solemn; it's downright cranky-looking. I am determined, over this season, to make him smile. Maybe I'll go back to the store and get one of those stone angels to help me. Or a laughing Buddha.

MIDSUMMER'S EVE

This is very midsummer madness.

—Shakespeare

Trees, though they are cut and lopped, grow up again quickly.

—Pericles

We inter-breathe with the rain forests, we drink from the oceans. They are part of our own body.

—Jack Kornfield

Mindful practice is simply the ongoing discovery of the thread of interconnectedness.

—Jon Kabat-Zinn

I always used to think that Midsummer's Eve, in the third week of June, came much too early in the season. It certainly was *not* the midpoint of my summer vacation from school, and technically, marked the *beginning* of summer. But it is, in fact, the middle of the calendar year, the summer solstice, and the longest day of the year.

From then on, the daylight hours decrease steadily until the winter solstice.

Since the first time I saw Shakespeare's *A Midsummer-Night's Dream* performed many years ago, I've always thought of the time as somehow magical. A night when fairies run about, getting into mischief, tricking and making fools of us mere mortals. I've since come across various folklore concerning Midsummer's Eve. This year, I tried to tell my daughter that if she put a saucer of flour under our rosemary bush at sunset on June 20, the next morning she'd find the initials of her future spouse etched in the flour. She wasn't interested. To my surprise, she didn't roll her eyes in that way she usually does when she thinks I'm being utterly ridiculous, that my ideas are either too New Age or too mainstream for her, depending on the situation. Instead, she simply said that she didn't want to know, that if she knew, it would always be in the back of her mind and the temptation to interfere would be too great. It would just screw things up somehow. Her innate understanding of the human ego is admirably extensive. Just letting life unfold is a true Zen attitude.

So there was no plate of flour under the rosemary bush when Midsummer's Eve descended upon our house. It was a very hot, humid, and quiet night. Or rather, I thought it was quiet because I couldn't hear anything over the racket made by my air conditioner. Its hum wove in and out of my dreams, like an insistent lullaby. I entrusted the night garden to the fairies and slept soundly.

Opening the back door to my garden in the morning, I was greeted by a completely unexpected and bizarre sight. A huge branch had fallen off the giant silver maple tree and was now resting on the fence along the back of my property. It looked like a giant hand, its fingers woven between the slats of the wooden fence (which miraculously had not fallen down under its weight), and its broken wrist reaching straight up into the air a few feet from the place where it had snapped off its long arm.

With no prior warning, this tree had begun pruning itself earlier in the season. One evening in late May, another large branch had suddenly fallen onto our neighbor's driveway. Luckily, no one was hurt and there were no cars in the driveway at the time. I found out later that it had happened shortly after someone I knew had died. It was a woman I had interviewed for a book I was writing and who had given me far more than I'd expected—a wonderful story that I felt deserved its own book, one I would write later. She died suddenly of a heart attack the night before the branch fell off my maple tree. I felt a shiver when I was told she had died and when. Had she visited me? Was she telling me to write the book anyway? I knew she had wanted to tell her story very much and had been looking for someone to write it for her. Always looking for portents and signs revealing the underlying mysteries of life, I had wondered about some possible connection between this woman's sudden death and the branch falling off my tree.

When the first branch had fallen, we thought we'd better have the tree looked at by a specialist, but we hadn't gotten around to it when the second branch fell. The tree was so large and beautiful, so full of fresh green leaves, that we couldn't believe there might be something wrong with it. We blamed the years of cutting and pruning that had been done to it in order to accommodate electrical and telephone wires. It had grown off in two opposite directions instead of straight up, and eventually the weight of the branches got to be too much. At least that's what we thought.

But the branch falling on Midsummer's Eve the way it did made me wonder. If it was the woman who had died suddenly before I'd finished writing her story, there seemed to be some sense of urgency about whatever message she was trying to get to me. *Pay attention!* the tree seemed to be screaming at me. But pay attention *to* what? I wondered. This was the first year since we'd moved into this house, five years ago, that I'd really started making the garden my own. I'd messed with some of the tree roots growing throughout the yard, but hardly enough to damage the tree. Were the fairies of the garden trying to tell me something? Or were they pruning the old tree to give the garden more sunlight?

When you believe, as I do, that there is a reason for everything, that everything means something on some (usually secret) level, you can't help but think of all these things to try to figure out the meaning, the message, the purpose hidden within everything that happens. At least the human ego can't help doing those things. But Zen means not thinking about all of that. It means quietly waiting for things to unfold and reveal themselves to you. It means being like my wise daughter, who doesn't want to be told the initials of her future husband.

The tree surgeon craned his neck up at the broken limbs. "How do you feel about this tree?" he asked. Responding to our quizzical expressions, he continued, "I mean, how much do you want to keep the tree? Because, eventually, it's going to have to come down." Our spirits sank along with our faces and shoulders. "Of course, *eventu-*

ally can be a long time in the life of a tree like this one." We agreed to let him cut most of the lower branches that shade our backyard, leaving only the tree's huge trunk and uppermost branches intact. Walking around the neighborhood, we noticed that many of the large old trees had been pruned in this manner, like stalks of broccoli that had been cleaned of all their lower leaves. We guessed that this was part of the necessary life cycle of such trees.

I dreamed of that woman whose story I hadn't had the chance to write before she died. In my dream, I was talking with her and then saying to my husband, "But she's dead. How could she be standing there talking to me?" It was a strange dream, full of that mix of confusion and clarity, fantasy and reality that only dreams can have. A loud crashing sound woke me up. I ran downstairs to look outside and see what had happened. Another maple—this one in front of my house, on the city park property—had dropped an enormous branch onto the street. The sound it had made—first a loud cracking and then the boom of hitting the ground—echoed in my mind, filling me with the strong sense that my house, and all of the human buildings and settlements around it, were situated in the middle of a natural forest. Whatever we did there, the forest continued living its natural life.

I thought a lot about the concept of energy and where it comes from and how it travels and what it does. It seemed that some sort of energy was flowing through what was left of the natural forest all around me. It wasn't in the form of a thunderstorm or wind or lightning; it was more subtle, but with just as powerful effects. Was it simply the age of the trees? Was it time for them to shed some large branches according to some secret calendar? Or was some specific energy surging around my house for some unknown reason?

Six months earlier, the main character in the story I was going to write about that woman had died. Now, only a few weeks after she had died, I heard that the third important person in the story was also dead. I wondered what happens to the energy in a living body when it dies. Does it fly away somewhere else? Does it go around breaking branches off big old trees? Does it simply dissipate into nothing? Was there an energy in all of my plants and trees that was somehow all connected to one another and to us humans?

The branch that had fallen on city property disappeared almost as soon as the sun came up. An efficient crew of workers made a clean cut where the limb had cracked off, chopped up the huge branch with their monster machinery, and hauled it away within an hour. We continued chopping the branches that had fallen in our backyard for weeks. We won't have to buy firewood this year.

The fairies running around the forest in which we have built our homes and cities have not left. They are the personification of the energy that connects us all. The energy that tells the trees to prune themselves is the same energy that tells me to write the story I have been given. The power that breaks off tree limbs is the same power that ends the lives of its individual manifestations. We are all part of this one big energy: plants, animals, people, earth, wind, and sky. On Midsummer's Eve the fairies romp, visiting our dreams and waking us up with a boom in the night. Every once in a while, we need to be reminded of the earth and air all around us, of the energy that surges everywhere and within us. Once a year, the fairies give us a little nudge, a tiny tap, a small poke to remind us once again that we are part of the infinite energy of life.

The interconnectedness of everything is the very core of Zen. The realization that we are not separate from the living universe, but an integral part of it, is correct Zen mindfulness. Experiencing our oneness with the stars, the trees, the birds, and the soil is central to Zen practice. There is nothing in the universe that has nothing to do with us, and nothing that is not affected by us. Like the squirrels that nest in the trees and trees themselves, we are each in our own way manifestations of the same single energy, the same living force, the same One Mind.

WALKING

When you walk, just walk.   —Yun-man

In those vernal seasons of the year, when the air is calm and pleasant, it were an injury and sullenness against Nature not to go out, and see her riches, and partake in her rejoicing with heaven and earth.
        —John Milton

The world cannot be discovered by a journey of miles, however long, but only by a spiritual journey, a journey of only one inch very arduous and humble and joyful, by which we arrive at the ground at our feet, and learn to be at home.
        —Wendell Berry

We can never get enough of nature.
—Henry David Thoreau

What continues to astonish me about a garden is that you can walk past it in a hurry, see something wrong, stop to set it right, and emerge an hour or two later breathless, contented, and wondering what on earth happened.
—Dorothy Gilman

I walk in my garden daily, several times if possible. I like to walk barefoot, feeling the grass beneath my feet, free to step into a flower bed or vegetable patch without worrying about getting my shoes wet or dirty. I just walk, looking and listening. I praise, ask, touch, smell, and commune with my garden. It always makes me feel good to walk through my garden, whether I'm tired, angry, or feeling stressed.

As a matter of fact, walking is all I really feel that I do in my garden. I never go out there with the thought, "I must weed now," or "I'm going to get to those gardening chores today." I don't approach my garden with day planners and to-do list in hand. I just walk in my garden and see what I see. Sometimes, a weed or a dead leaf or a ripe vegetable calls out to be picked; a tomato vine needs to be tied up to its stake; drooping impatiens want water. I let the garden tell me what to do and I just do it. Weeding, picking, transplanting, watering, and all the other work that gardening consists of are things I simply don't think about; they're not chores or problems. If they happen to be there when I'm walking in the garden, I deal with them then and there.

Walking in my garden, I just walk. I see, hear, touch, and smell. I taste my steaming cup of morning coffee. No thinking, no reasoning, no judging anything. Everything just is as it is. I open the gate and step onto the grass. It is cool and wet with dew. My toe stumbles on a bit of root protruding from the ground; the giant trees stretch their roots for yards around them. The air is fresh and cool, blowing lightly across my skin. The wind chime makes soft, melodic sounds. I see the velvety purple petals of the impatiens, their green leaves, the deep brown earth in which they grow. The hosta are blooming in a lighter bluish purple, tall stalks with delicate blossoms hanging downward all along their height. The heartease smile in purple and yellow faces. I am aware of a vast variety of shades and hues of the color green. Bright yellow blossoms peek through the fuzzy, sticky leaves and thick stems of the zucchini plants. The lettuce stands thick in yet another, paler shade of green. The tomato plants are now almost as tall as I am. The tiny yellow flowers have turned to multitudes of small green fruit, in various shapes and sizes: cherry, plum, and big, gently ribbed spheres. The scent of basil and marigolds accompanies them. An airplane flies overhead. A car engine starts in the distance. I run my hands through the rosemary bush and breathe in the delicious, soapy aroma. Mint, oregano, sage, and chives drift through my consciousness, leaving a potpourri of scent. The marigolds are filled with large orange blossoms. A squirrel scurries across the top of the fence, a green crabapple sticking out of his mouth. I sip my coffee, cooler now, sweet and rich tasting. The grass beneath my feet is still cool and wet. I bend down close to the ground and catch the scent of onions and garlic, light and sweet, emanating from the earth.

As I walk through my garden, I pop the deadheads off the marigolds, pull weeds here and there, fix this and change that. I never tire of gardening because I never make a chore out of it. I just walk, and along the way, I reach in and help a little, too. I focus all of my attention—open, alert, receptive, and humble—on my garden, and whatever needs doing simply gets done through me. I realize how much time we spend thinking about the past and future, instead of being where we are when we're there. Walking in my garden, I am nowhere but right here, right now, part of everything around me.

In our culture, we tend to be time-oriented. We eat, sleep, work, play, bathe, and make love when it's time for those things. We are ruled by our day planners, paying more attention to our schedules than to the activities listed in them. If we skip a lunch or coffee break because we're so absorbed in our work, we often can't take another one when it's more convenient. Slaves to our clocks, we do everything in a hurry, while thinking about getting on to the next thing.

In Zen, the concept of self is something we try to get past. While it may seem that keeping very busy is a way of losing ourselves, it is really a way of being self-absorbed and self-important. Our true essential nature is to work when there is work to be done and rest when we are tired. It is being fully, completely, totally aware of each present moment as it happens. It means realizing in everything we do that we are connected to everything else in the universe. It is attentiveness, focus, and concentration. While some of us are fortunate enough to find this kind of losing ourselves in the work we do, in dance, sports, painting, or music, the garden offers us all a relatively easy, available opportunity to learn what it means to truly lose ourselves in something else.

When I walk in my garden, I consider it a Zen practice. I go without any agenda, without motives or objectives or any purpose other than just walking. Often, all that happens is that I walk, I see, I hear, I smell. Sometimes, I follow the energy of the plants and participate a little in their living and growing. I don't force anything, or decide anything, or do anything. I just walk in my garden, and what happens, happens. This practice requires openness and attention, and gives back peace and joy.

Sometimes, we get caught up in trying to do Zen practice the same way we try to do everything else: quickly, competitively, following schedules and rules. We think that maybe we shouldn't reach in and pick that weed, because, after all, we're supposed to be just walking and nothing else. Instead of losing ourselves, we lose our true focus and attention. Rather than letting the moment tell us what it is, we try to force whatever we think a Zen moment should be. We think walking shouldn't turn into weed-picking or harvesting vegetables or watering plants. And sometimes, it won't. But when it does, we can let go and give in and be fully in the present moment, whatever it brings. The only right way to just walk in our garden is openly, peacefully, and attentively.

For a few minutes this morning, I focused completely on the simple act of walking in my garden and felt totally at one with it. I picked a few weeds, popped the deadheads off a few marigolds and petunias, and smelled the herbs. I heard the sounds of cicadas, birds, and traffic outside my fence. I felt the dew on my feet, the air on my skin, and the breath in my body. I started the day feeling fully connected to and part of nature—just walking in my garden.

LIFE CYCLES

At Christmas I no more desire a rose
Than wish a snow in May's newfangled mirth;
But like of each thing that in season grows.
                                        —William Shakespeare

To every thing there is a season, and a time for every
purpose under heaven.

                                        —Ecclesiastes 3:1

Green beans and lettuce have relatively short maturing times, so I can always plant two successive crops of them, even in the brief growing season where I live. They accomplish their purpose quickly. The tiny sprouts appear very soon after planting the seeds in shallow soil, and in the case of lettuce, what begins growing then is all there is to the vegetable—it just gets larger. In the case of the bush bean, stalks only grow to be about a foot high, leaves stretch out to cover and shade the tiny white blossoms that foretell the beans themselves. Suddenly, they are laden with ripe, crisp green beans, ready to eat. Both lettuce and beans are delicious raw, fresh from the garden.

The abundance of these vegetables fills us with summer joy as well as nourishment. When my daughter was small, she could often be found happily munching a bean straight off the bush, while playing in the garden. The lettuce is tender and sweet, giving us many wonderful salads and adding a crisp, buttery sweetness to our sandwiches.

When these plants mature, they begin to look a little weathered. The oldest leaves begin to yellow and wither. Their robust strength turns to frail weakness. They have given up their life and vitality to the food we take from them. Their remains come up easily by the roots, making way for a new batch of plants and blossoms and food. They have fulfilled their purpose, beautifully and bountifully.

Other plants in my garden vary in their life span over a season. Some flourish early and fade in the hot summer sun. Others grow slowly and steadily over a long period of months. Some appear idle for times, and then have sudden bursts of growth. All are fulfilling their true purpose, their essential nature. Many plants in the garden offer us far more than we know how to use. Herbal remedies and cosmetics, edible flowers, and even just seeds that could be saved for next year's garden often waste away in the garden and compost heap. Even the psychological and emotional benefits of aromatic plants are overlooked and wasted. But the ebb and flow of nature's abundance continues, whatever uses we do or do not make of it.

The ebb and flow of all natural things, of all life, is a constant of our earth. Cycles of birth, growth, and death continuously flow through time. Ascent and decline, abundance and barrenness, take their turns over and over and over again. Life is change. What is barren will fill with abundance; what is abundant will become barren. What is lush and green will turn yellow and brown; what is laden with fruit will give up its fruit and begin again, in one form or another. What is young will become old. What is alive will die.

One of my cats died early this morning. It was very sudden and unexpected, although she was an old cat, as cats go. We got her about twelve years ago, when she was a tiny kitten, from someone I worked with whose cat had a large litter. She and one other littermate were the last kittens to find homes. We'd only planned on taking one, since we were a little concerned about our Siberian husky, a gentle and loving dog who wasn't quite aware of her own size and strength. But when we went to pick one up, we found these two tiny sisters, mewing frantically, shivering with fright, hiding under the furniture together. We took them both home, although capturing them took a bit of doing. They mewed loudly all the way home, clutching the backseat of the car with their little needlelike claws.

I suppose their terror was what had made the two kittens the least desirable of the litter, the hardest to place in loving, happy homes. But we felt so bad for them, we thought they might be a little less afraid if they stayed together. We also worried about what would happen to them if we didn't take them. My coworker would have turned them over to the animal shelter, where they'd really be frightened and probably unadoptable. We were sure these tiny, helpless, but very healthy creatures would be euthanised.

At home, we confined the kittens to a small area to give them time to get used to us and their new home. The dog was very curious, sniffing and dancing around at the doorway, her ears perked up at the unfamiliar sound of mewing. Gradually, we allowed them to meet one another, and they quickly formed their own animal family. The big dog would often sit down with a kitten between her outstretched front legs, licking the little creature until her fur stood up, wet and spiky. One kitten liked to climb up the screen door to our backyard, until her claws grew too big to grasp the wire mesh.

Our animal family grew up along with our human one. Over the years, each animal's individual personality emerged. The husky grew from our young daughter's playmate to the cats' mother. Anastasia, the all-black cat, was reclusive by nature, but came out of hiding for a daily dose of cuddling and conversation with her animal and human families. Natasha, the tabby, attached herself to our daughter, sleeping on her bed at night—and most of the day—and flopping belly-up on the rug at the back door every afternoon when our daughter came home from school.

After several years of this harmonious family life, the dog fell ill. For several months, we took her to the vet's regularly and treated her at home as her fur fell out and her legs lost the strength to carry her body. She'd crawl into the cool shade under our deck and then be unable to get herself back out. She grew increasingly incontinent. Eventually, the vet convinced us that the quality of her life was not going to improve, and the kindest thing to do would be to put the dog out of her misery. After saying our good-byes to this loving creature who had been a member of our family for eleven years, we stood over her lifeless body and cried. We saw tears in the eyes of her lifelong doctor and his assistant, too.

While our cats, who by then numbered three, couldn't tell us what they were thinking or feeling, they seemed to us to wander about the house mewing more than usual, looking for the dog. They had certainly witnessed her long decline (in that way cats have of providing their comforting presence to the sick) and had contributed to whatever quality of life she'd had to the end. One year later, we brought home a Samoyed puppy, and it was the cats' turn to be the mothers and bosses of the house. Perhaps that is why this dog has retained her puppyishness throughout her six years of life.

Tasha showed no signs of illness before her death early this morning. She was an old cat, no longer very active, and slow-moving, but the only warning we'd had that something was wrong was that one of the cats—we didn't know which one—hadn't quite made it all the way to the litter box before relieving herself twice in the past two days. We looked each of the cats over, but saw nothing unusual in their appearance or behavior. Yesterday, Tasha lolled contentedly on my husband's stomach as he napped on the sofa. Her loud purring could be heard across the room.

At about midnight last night, our daughter (home for the summer from college) went downstairs for a snack and found Tasha crawling behind a radiator, mewing loudly and constantly. We managed to pull her out from there, where we discovered she had relieved her bowels. She lay stretched out on the rug, still mewing and immobile. We found the emergency animal hospital's phone number and called. They told us to bring the cat right in.

The clinic was very clean and pleasant, everything new-looking and well-equipped. The staff was warm and loving toward the animals, and clear and communicative with their human companions. A father and son were there before us, having brought in a stray cat they had found which had been hit by a car. It wasn't even their cat, and they were at the animal ER in the middle of the night, spending God knew how much money to try to save the cat's life. We liked this place.

But Tasha progressed quickly from bad to worse in the hour we spent there, experiencing several seizures and finally arresting. There was nothing they could do for her. We leaned over her as she lay under the heat lamp, covered with a colorful towel, stroked her fur, and said our good-byes. We realized that she hadn't really been aware of our presence the whole time we were at the vet's; we could see in her eyes that she had already left us. She had called us to find her and say good-bye back at home. Again, we cried. But we were comforted by the long and happy life we knew she had lived, all the love she had received from her animal and human families. We knew she hadn't suffered much or long. Her life cycle was complete.

If the purpose of lettuce and bean plants is food, what was the purpose of a cat that was not even expected to keep a house or barn mouse-free? The purpose of Tasha's life was simply love. She helped to fill the lives of three people and four other animals with sweetness, gentleness, kindness, affection, and playfulness. She helped my daughter's upbringing and education include love and respect for animals. She was at least part of the reason we are all now vegetarians.

Tasha's life also taught us about the ebb and flow of life's energy. What is young will become old; what is abundant will seem to disappear; what is alive will die. What sometimes seems to us to be the cruelty of nature is simply the natural and inevitable ebb and flow of all things in life. We gain, we lose; we go, we stop; we give, we receive;

we have, and we let go. Life isn't cruel, it just is what it is. All we can do about it is to make the most of what we have when we have it and to let it go when the time comes. Abundance will come again. Strength, growth, vitality, love, and abundance are all around us, always. And so are decline, barrenness, and death. Every life has its seasons.

The continuous ebb and flow of life creates balance in nature. Balance creates harmony, and harmony is the essential nature of life. All living things are in constant change. Birth, growth, and death are the way of this world. All of these cycles support each other. And they teach us about joy and sadness, optimism and acceptance, beginnings and endings.

In August some flowers are in full bloom; others are losing their color, strength, and vitality; and still others are long gone. Plants and trees bear fruit, and in doing so, give up some of their life, their nourishment, their vital force. Vegetables are harvested, their mother vines tossed onto the compost heap. The strong heat and sunshine bring some plants to their fullest life potential and wither others. This ebb and flow of life energy continues around and within us every moment of every day. Tides that are going out in one place are flowing in someplace else. Life on our earth is an intricate lace of strong thread and empty spaces. Both are essential to the whole cloth. Each gives the other its life. Together, they maintain the endless, living universe.

The ebb and flow of life makes us richer in experience and understanding, in our abilities to love, enjoy, accept, hold on, and let go. Abundance means more when we truly understand barrenness; life means more when death reaches close to us. We can experience both the ebb and the flow more fully, more mindfully, and more gratefully, knowing that neither could exist without the other.

THE PINE TREES

*In the beginner's mind
there are many possibilities.
In the expert's mind
there are few.*

—Shunryu Suzuki

*Just live with it for a while. Watch it the way you
watch a line when fishing and before long, as sure as
you live, you'll get a little nibble, a little fact asking
in a timid, humble way if you're interested in it.*

—Robert M. Pirsig

There are two huge pine trees in my front garden, between the street and the hill on which my house rests. I have no way of knowing exactly how long they have stood there, but surely longer than the old house has been here and longer than I have been alive. They stand guard over the property like two sentries, watching, listening, softening the wind and snow and noise from the street below before it reaches the house.

These two tall trees created a large bare patch beneath and between them: barren earth covered with pine needles, cones, and fallen branches. The lower limbs of the trees had been removed, making this patch highly visible to all who pass by. It was an unsightly patch. "Nothing can grow there," was the comment most often heard from my elderly neighbors as they walked past, watching me clear away the debris for the umpteenth time.

I wanted to somehow work *with* these trees, to create an aesthetically pleasing space together. I decided to look at the area as if for the first time. I let go of the visions I'd had of what I wished I could grow there, what would be nice, if only . . . I accepted what I had been given to work with—intense shade, cooler temperatures, pine needles that would continue falling—and I waited. I waited for it to tell me what to do, what it needed and wanted and what wanted to be there. As I cut the grass around it, watered and pruned and planted its neighboring plants and trees, the space stayed in the back of my mind and the corner of my eye, until it was ready.

The overall shape of the space gradually revealed itself to me. Why hadn't I seen it before? If clearly defined by some kind of border, it created a very pleasing kidney shape. I suddenly remembered the tons of hosta plants I had growing in my back garden that loved shade and could easily be split into many smaller plants. They were perfect border plants, with a thickness of large dark green leaves growing close to the ground and sending one thin stalk of delicate blue-purple flowers up into the air in midsummer. They weren't top-heavy plants, like gladiolus, which fall over as soon as their flowers bloom, begging to be cut and brought indoors. The tall shoots of light blossoms stood straight up reaching for the sky, like the pines themselves.

I dug a trench around the pines in a soft, natural shape and began moving the hosta plants from their home in my back garden. At first I tried to be very careful not to hurt their roots, tangled and entwined as they were from growing up together for many years. But after a while, I realized that I could not avoid cutting them somewhere and ending up with mixed roots. One of my curious neighbors laughed at my concern and said, "Oh, cut 'em anywhere! They don't care. They'll always come back, those hostas." And I did. Not carelessly, but trustingly. I separated them into many smaller clumps of long, round leaves and put them in the ground under the pines. They re covered nicely with just a little time and care, and even seemed to enjoy their new home. They formed a long, lazy ring around the bare spot, setting it off from the rest of the land. Suddenly, attention was drawn clearly to the area I had wanted to make disappear. And it called me to work with it.

Not really knowing what I was going to do, I began turning over the soil, mixing the dry, brown pine needles with the dirt that lay underneath. Surprised by the richness of the heavy clay soil, I dug deeper. Digging and turning, digging and turning, the covering of needles blended with and lightened the dark, secret earth that had lain untouched for years. Together, they created a new earth—new color, new texture, new substance—ready for new growth and new life.

As I dug and turned, dug and turned, I thought about how certain I had been that nothing like this could ever be uncovered here, that "Nothing can grow there," as my neighbor had said. My mind drifted to images of the urban apartment I had once lived in, surrounded by concrete and brick. I'd hung window boxes and grown flowers, herbs, and even tomatoes in them. There was a tiny patch of earth next to one of the buildings on my courtyard—it couldn't have been more than two feet by four—where various neighbors had planted a flower here, a patio tomato plant there, and even a cannabis plant had appeared from an unnamed contributor. What little bit of earth we had at our disposal, we had each used to the fullest.

I thought, too, of my own grandmother, who had worked the small plot of land in the backyard of her urban house for thirty-some years. It was a haven rich with scents that gave as much pleasure as the wonderful tastes in store at harvest time. It was a kingdom of flowers and herbs, vegetables and grass. My grandmother used to talk about—and to—her plants as if they were people, chiding the mint for always trying to take over, brushing the tops of the basil's "heads," telling them how lovely they were, how well they were growing, and breathing deeply the rich aroma they left clinging to her hands. When she sold her house and moved into a condo without any earth at all to work with, I thought that was the end of all that gardening for her, and for me to visit and enjoy. But her tiny concrete balcony was soon overflowing with potted tomatoes, basil, mint, peppers, beans, and much more.

The digging and turning became a kind of meditative practice, my body a rhythmic part of all that surrounded me. The soil, the pine needles, the trees, the hosta—it was all part of me and I was part of it. I began believing—without thinking about it consciously—that I would know what to do when the time came to do it. I stopped trying to have a plan for this space, but to just let it happen. I knew that all my thinking about what I had wanted to change, to hide, to dig up and cart away, could never create whatever the natural intention was for this space. I just let myself blend in with it. Like the bees and butterflies and birds and squirrels, I just did what felt like my part. I stopped thinking at all, and just dug and turned, dug and turned.

Living Zen, in the garden or anywhere else, doesn't mean that we do nothing; it means that everything we do flows from our true natural being and is harmonious with the true natural being of everything else. We don't push, force, or manipulate; instead, we become one with our surroundings and add our positive energy to them.

I sat under the pine trees to rest. A man walked by briskly, fitting his exercise routine into his obviously busy day. His gait was quick and purposeful; earphone wires hung from his ears to a little black box somehow fastened to his matching sweats; and he held a book in his hands, reading as he walked. He didn't see me; he didn't see anything. Walking, listening, reading: Was he really doing any of them? I was reminded to just sit, to concentrate fully on where I was and what I was doing every moment. I felt the cool air under the trees, ran my fingers through the dry soil and pine needles I had been turning over, and breathed the fresh, clean scent of pine as I listened to the rustling song of the branches over my head.

My mind floated back to another garden I'd had at a different house. I had planted new shrubbery in front of the building and the clean, rich soil around them had looked bare. I'd thought of spreading stones or wood chips around the base of the bushes I'd planted, but I didn't really want to spend the money and preferred a natural ground cover. But what would grow in the cool, dark, shady space beneath my shrubs? A neighbor of mine had suggested ajuga, a purple, velvety ground cover that grows anywhere, sending shoots out all around it and spreading itself aggressively. I'd imbedded a wooden border around the shrub area to keep the ajuga from spreading into my lawn.

I had a little ajuga now, somewhere on my property, but it wasn't much, and it had to be separated into enough small plants to fill the space beneath the pines. As I worked at splitting the plants and spacing them out throughout the area, I began seeing in my mind a beautiful purple velvet carpet under these trees. The border of hosta had already created a soft, rounded shape, like an oasis, under the trees. I thought of their tall, delicate flowers that would shoot up later in the season, ringing the area with a short, natural fence. I remembered that ajuga, too, produced shorter blue flowers much earlier in the season. I envisioned the purple carpet topped with a sea of tiny blue flowers in the early spring, followed by the hosta blossoms, pulling up the edges of the space, as the center gently sank back to its ground-hugging level.

But something was missing. The vision I'd had of what the space would look like when the plants had taken hold and spread was lovely, balanced, and pleasing to the eye. But something called my attention to the very center of the space. After a few days of planting ajuga, a thought came to me. The space created between the pines was triangular, pointing upward toward the hill in front of the house. The number three kept running through my mind. There are three of us in my family; mind, body, and soul . . . I felt the sense of trinity already existing in the center of the space, and it called out to me. I had another variety of hosta that was larger than what I'd used for the border, and I planted three of them right in the center of the space between the two pines. I placed one behind and two in front, creating a triangular shape that pointed upward between the trees. I knew instantly that my work was finished.

Two years later, I watched the garden beneath the two pines unfold. First, the infant greenery forming the border and the center focal point; then the baby ajuga, dark green at first, sending its shoots out in all directions, claiming the space as its own. The green turns to rich velvety purple and then rises up in a flurry of tiny blue blossoms that settle back down again softly, while the hosta rises up around the border, forming a protective ring around it all. Finally, the big round ball of green at the center shoots out three thick stems, tall and proud, and blue blossoms burst forth.

It's an annual process that continues with almost no help from me. Nothing needs to be planted or coaxed into living there. Nothing needs to be kept up in order to maintain an unnatural setup. The pine needles fall, creating a natural mulch holding the moisture in the soil and nourishing the ajuga and hosta plants. Everything is as it was meant to be. The process goes on without me. I was just a little part of it for a little time. And it rewards me with its beauty year after year. I look at it and remember the barren spot of dirt and pine needles where "nothing could grow," and I am reminded not to think I know so much before I even start something. When you start out with beginner's mind, anything is possible.

MY GARDEN, MYSELF

A garden that one makes oneself becomes associated with one's personal history and that of one's friends, interwoven with one's tastes, preferences, and character, and constitutes a sort of unwritten, but withal manifest, autobiography. Show me your garden, provided that it be your own, and I will tell you what you are like.

—Alfred Austin

The work of a garden bears visible fruits—in a world where most of our labours seem suspiciously meaningless.

—Pam Brown

Every flower about a house certifies to the refinement of somebody. Every vine climbing and blossoming tells of love and joy.

—Robert G. Ingersoll

Our gardens reflect us in many ways. They manifest aspects as diverse as our tastes and preferences, our backgrounds and experiences, our time and budget constraints. They also tell of our self-image and the image we wish to project outward to the world. They show our strengths and weaknesses, manifested in earth and greenery. They tell the world some things about us, and they tell us some things about ourselves.

I like to walk and drive around, looking at other people's gardens. At first, of course, I tend to judge them all: *That one looks pretty, that one looks strained and uptight; that one looks wild and abundant, that one neglected. . . .* But after a while, I stop judging them and just look at them. They all start seeping into my consciousness as images: color, shape, texture, scent. My mind fills up with an abundance of these images, all blending together as one: life, nature, beauty. Garden images nourish my hungry mind and heart and soul: food, medicine, love.

You can tell a lot about a person by looking at his or her garden. And yet, here we are again, in danger of making judgments. We tend to assume and decide things about what we think we see reflected in someone's flower beds and vegetable patches. But if we let ourselves get past that judgmental stage, we again move on to just seeing. We see gardens created and attended by human beings. We see the effects of human beings on their natural surroundings, our interaction with the earth. We see the blending of plants, soil, air, sunshine, water, and people.

When we see a garden that is loved by someone, we can feel it instantly—if we are open to feeling it. It goes far beyond the pleasing placement of plants or some properly followed rules. It just is. The love leaps out at us and connects with us in a most fundamental and natural way. It has nothing to do with intellectual judgments, prize-winning flowers, or perfect fruits and vegetables. Such a garden reflects the heart and soul of its human member, and speaks directly to the heart and soul within each of us.

We can also see fear and self-doubt revealed in our gardens. Depression and sorrow can make us neglect our gardens (although I suspect gardening could provide a brilliant tonic for these, if we managed to force ourselves to begin). Carelessness, hopelessness, resignation, and laziness appear in the forms of drab, dreary plots of brown grass and weeds. We can see the transformation of a garden when ownership changes hands: in one season, a hillside of wild brush is cleared and suddenly becomes a lovely haven of straight trees, lush greenery, bright red flowers, robust green melons, and yellow squash; another new resident lets an overworked triangle of land grow completely wild, creating a sanctuary of wildflowers and tall grasses for small animals, birds, and insects.

The diversity of the gardens I see amazes me. One small urban house is buffered from the busy street by a thick plot of tall and colorful flowers filling the entire yard inside a chain-link fence; the neighbors' grassy lawns on either side look barren by comparison. A suburban home on a hill is surrounded by terraced levels of flower beds; dozens of varieties and colors mixed in a brilliant and beautiful jumble. Down the street, a beige house with a closely cut lawn is encircled with an expanse of beige stones, punctuated at regular intervals by large pink geraniums; no other vegetation or color can be seen anywhere on the property. Window boxes overflow with ivies and petunias; blue morning glories and purple clematis wind their way up fences, trellises, and lampposts; bright yellow daylilies line walkways; and daisies reach their proud heads above crowds of snapdragons and salvia. Vegetables grow as well in front of houses as in back. None of this is wild or natural. People do all of these things, and so much more, with whatever portion of land they call their own.

I find myself forming images of the people who may live in these homes and tend these gardens: their ages and lifestyles, their jobs, children (or no children), and personalities. These are all assumptions, of course. I really don't know the people who belong to these gardens. But certain attributes associate themselves with the pictures formed by the nature growing around these homes: cold, hot, sterile, messy, happy, sad, relaxed, free, uptight, wild, natural, artificial, offbeat, and creative, to name only a few. In some gardens, you can easily imagine children and dogs playing, people laughing, cooking aromas drifting out through the open kitchen windows; other settings are clearly designed for quietly watching a sunset or reading a book. Still others appear either lonely and neglected or whipped into shape by a firm, unyielding hand.

You can feel something of the gardener's relationship with nature in his or her garden. Our relationship with nature seems also to reflect our relationship with many other things and with life itself. If it is true that we are, physically, what we eat, then perhaps in some ways we are also our gardens—emotionally, psychologically, and spiritually. How we approach gardening may have something to say about how we approach everything else in life. And what we create there may have something to tell us about ourselves.

People rarely live in one spot all of their lives anymore, so our gardens often reflect only certain periods in our lives, specific selves that we are or have been. My garden this year only tells something of who I am right now, in this stage of my life. Other gardens I have grown have told very different stories. Other people's gardens may, at least partially, reflect how long they have lived with them, while also containing remnants of other gardeners who have lived there before them. So no garden reflects one person's heart and soul purely. But all of that history is part of the garden that exists today, and which parts we choose to keep or tear up and replace is part of our garden's story about us.

In my observations of gardens, I have not neglected the professionally tended institutional ones. The conservatory, arboretum, and public rose garden all reflect the scientific study of their caretakers and the eternal human quest for the perfect specimen. The professionally landscaped professional building projects an image of clean, crisp efficiency. These gardens tend to reflect human ideas or ideals, rather than personality traits or emotions. We can appreciate them on an intellectual level, but they don't really touch us on that level of heart and soul, because they have not been created by and infused with the heart and soul—only the work—of another human being.

When I return home and look again at my own garden, I see far more than what is tangibly visible. I see the previous owners of the property and their professional landscaper. I see all the trials and errors that I have made in this season, and all the incarnations of the five seasons we have lived here. I see plants I would not have chosen this year if they had not been given to me as gifts. I see all the plants I'd thought of and planned on planting in my garden, but which, for one reason or another, did not end up here. I see all the various stages of my planning for this year's garden and all my new plans for next year.

No stranger looking at my garden could see all of that. A stranger couldn't know about the tiny maple tree my daughter discovered growing wild and nurtured and replanted so that it would grow straight and later moved from the side to the front of the house. They wouldn't be able to see the Japanese yews that died on either side of the front steps and had to be removed, or the dead, empty space beneath the pine trees that's now filled with hosta encircling viny ground covers. They'd never guess at the beds of impatiens behind my previous house or my grandmother's vegetable garden, both of which I have tried to recreate here. All of that and so much more are here for only my eyes to see. My garden is an extension of my self.

What anyone might see, if they really looked, is the large space devoted to vegetables. A forest of six-foot tomato plants overshadows their side of the garden. While the square footage of the two raised beds of lettuce, beans, carrots, zucchini, cucumbers, onions, eggplants, and tomatoes, plus the strip of herbs, is probably equal to or less than that of the flower beds, their presence is powerful. Planting perennials is relatively new to me, but my comfort and experience with vegetables and annuals is obvious. They might also notice that, with the exception of bright orange marigolds among my vegetables and herbs, my flowers all fall into the pink-blue-purple range of colors; red, yellow, and orange are completely absent from my perennial patch.

Like me, my garden is not perfect. It has its weak areas, failed experiments, and empty spaces. Its flowers bloom with vigor and splendor in some places and wither in others. The soil in spots is rich and full of nourishment, while in other spots it needs to be added to and built up before anything can take root and grow there. Overall, it reflects my own willingness to go just so far and then quit, give up, and turn back. It represents both my artistic and practical sides; my attempt to feed both body and soul, sometimes neglecting one for the sake of the other. It illustrates my split attention, the constant juggling act that is my life.

But I also see in my garden the universals of my humanity, the potentials and possibilities. I see that what I love flourishes, while what I merely tolerate withers. I see that everything, given what it needs to grow and thrive, will grow and thrive. I see that everything has its time of full blooming and its time of decline and death. I see not just the places where I am weak and barren, but also the places where I blossom into brilliant leaves and bold flowers. I begin to understand and accept that the vine must suffer for the sake of producing a bounty of healthy fruit.

My garden is constantly changing, evolving, and improving. It will never reach some ideal picture of perfection. Like me—and like all living things—it will always keep growing into something new and different, never stagnating. That nature moves ever forward is manifested equally in gardens and in people. My garden is never exactly the same from one year to the next, and neither am I.

In Zen, we try to lose ourselves—let go of our personal identities and just *be* within the whole of the universe—in order to find truth and reality. When we lose ourselves in gardening, we find ourselves reflected in our gardens. We are shown who we are, if we choose to look. We discover the truth and reality of our being, manifested in stems and flowers and vegetables. In Zen, we learn that everything in the world is a metaphorical representation of some higher truth. In our garden, we learn that everything in nature is a metaphor for something in us, and that what is in us is the whole universe. We are nature, nature is us; we are both the metaphor and what it represents, the reflection and the reality. We are the drop of water and the whole ocean. I lose myself in my garden and discover who I truly am.

IN GOOD COMPANY

Although the variety of natural things is so dazzlingly vast that no one color, sound, shape, or odor, however minute, is quite like any other, all natural things belong together just as they are.
—James P. Carse

There are myriad relationships continually going on unseen beneath the surface of the garden.
—Bob Flowerdew

It is quite true that eggplants next to potatoes will be more attractive to the potato beetle than the potatoes are: that zinnias (especially in white or pale colors), white roses and white geraniums will lure Japanese beetles away from other plants; and that dill charms that tomato hornworm into deserting the tomatoes. What of it? What of the eggplants, zinnias, white roses, dill, I have lost in the process?
—Eleanor Perenyi

In nature, things grow together where they are. One of the effects we humans have had on this earth is that we have moved a lot of things around. We have traveled the world over, learned from one another, and transplanted what we have found. On a smaller scale, we have brought certain lovely flowers and delectable fruits and vegetables into our gardens to grow where they never would have naturally. We have had a great deal of success in this, adapting (as humans are expert at doing) our varieties and hybrids to various climates and conditions.

And so, amazingly, I can grow tropical tomatoes and peppers for a few months each year, here in the cold northern United States. I can grow grapes, roses, and basil as easily as grass. It's hard to know how much of what we have become accustomed to growing in our own backyards is actually native to the area. We can grow almost anything we choose, at least for the warmer months of the year, almost anywhere.

However, each of these plants has an essential, original nature, wherever it is. If it is the true nature of a plant to grow in a tropical climate, the chances are not good that it will survive a Minnesota winter. Likewise, the natural friends and enemies of varieties of plant species do not change simply because we move the plant. People do not try to live under the same roof with bears or swim with sharks in their swimming pools. If you are allergic to a certain plant, you don't grow a crop of it in your backyard. Respect for the original, essential nature of all living things allows us to share the earth harmoniously.

Nature has seen fit to make certain plants enhance the health and happiness of certain others, and some plants are antagonistic toward one another. Also, some plants attract butterflies or birds, while others repel certain insects, giving their placement a strategic aspect. We take care to give our plants the right amount of sunlight and water, the right kind of soil and nutrients; why wouldn't we take into consideration the effect each of these plants has on the other? Learning about the various preferences and qualities of our plants can help us a great deal in planning our own gardens. An understanding of the true nature of the various members of our garden community enables us to be a more actively helpful participant in the life of the garden.

I learned early, in my grandmother's garden, that mint tends to spread insistently and must be planted in its own little world, where it can reign supreme. Tomato plants love basil and parsley planted among them, and garlic keeps many unpleasant insects out of the garden. Over the years, I learned in my own garden about the infinite benefits of marigolds, which repel all kinds bugs and weeds in both air and soil. They also smell great, and popping off their dead flowers keeps them blooming beautifully all summer long.

This year, I learned a new lesson the hard way. I had never thought about it before, but had always grown my tomatoes and peppers in separate parts of the garden. This year, I put my tomato plants in a raised bed with basil, eggplant, onions, and both green and red varieties of peppers. The whole bed was edged with a border of short, thick orange marigolds. I thought this was a perfect combination, since all of these plants love lots of heat and sunshine, and the marigolds would keep away leaf-eating aphids and nematodes that damage roots. I put them in the sunniest spot in my backyard. They all took root and grew for a while, but soon the peppers developed a spotty browning on their leaves. The leaves became misshapen and shriveled before any blossoms had even appeared.

I read everything I could find on the subject, and thought the problem looked like it might be something called mosaic, a virus spread by tomato-loving aphids. For the first time, I read that peppers should never be planted with tomatoes for this reason. Maybe the plants were infected before I bought them, or maybe the marigolds hadn't had enough time to take control of the garden away from insect pests. I tried every remedy I read about, from spraying the pepper plants with soapy water to planting petunias and garlic in between them, but it was too late. I ended up pulling up all my pepper plants, and it was too late in the season to plant new ones.

Usually, I enjoy the hit-or-miss, trial-and-error method of gardening; experimenting and learning things for myself. I like being free and creative in my garden, rather than learning how to do things someone else's way and then just copying them. But I really do miss having those peppers growing in my garden this year. I wish I had known more about the essential nature of peppers, tomatoes, aphids, and this mosaic thing. I wish I had considered companion planting a little bit more.

I'd thought about a lot of things when I planned and started my garden: the amount and direction of sunlight, the temperature difference between sunny and shady locations, soil depth and conditions, even the proximity to pine trees dropping their needles or maples dropping seed pods. I thought I'd covered it all. I'd thought enough about companion planting to know a few tips for what was good for my various plantings, but I admit I hadn't given much thought to what might be bad for them. Original nature is always a balance of both of these aspects.

We usually spend a lot of time and effort on what our gardens look like. We wonder if it's okay to mix certain colors or varieties of flowers; which plants will grow taller and therefore belong behind the shorter ones; whether there's any sort of danger in mixing flowers and vegetables. We wouldn't want to do anything stupid, like causing our pepper plants to self-destruct, but we love to break rules and exercise our creativity in the garden by putting things wherever we feel like putting them. Visually, that's exactly what we should do. We don't need to consult color wheels or follow preplanned designs from books or magazines to know where to put things. Nothing natural can clash; all that matters is that we like what we see.

However, where our plants would grow best is a different matter than where they might look best. Certain plants take certain elements out of the soil and put others back. One plant may attract the very insects that are the natural enemy of another plant. To learn all the possible combinations for better or worse, we'd all have to be scientists. But most of us aren't; we're gardeners. And that's something quite different. We bring more heart than science to what we do in the garden. So a lot of the choices we make are based on intuition and personal preference. Sometimes they work out great, and sometimes they don't.

I had to accept the loss of my pepper plants and appreciate the way the petunias, eggplants, marigolds, garlic, and onions filled in the space where they had been. It was really the only big companion planting mistake I seem to have made in my garden this year. Ironically, the more I have learned about companion planting, the more free I feel to mix different varieties together. Who would have thought to plant sunflowers with cucumbers? Or sweet-scented rosemary with carrots? Or morning glories climbing up stalks of sweet corn?

Over the years, I will expand my garden and the varieties of flowers, vegetables, and herbs I will attempt to grow. I will try to remember to keep daffodils away from tulips and tulips away from my lilacs. I will not grow lavender anywhere near my cucumbers, but I may plant some sage and hyssop throughout the vegetables. When I have enough room to grow sunflowers and sweet corn, I'll grow them together and let them be natural trellises for morning glories and runner beans. If I ever get around to trying my hand at roses, they will be accompanied by plenty of garlic. I will remember that the original nature of every living thing includes some natural friends and enemies.

Next year, I think I'll mix some daylilies in with my irises, dill with my lettuce and cucumbers, chamomile with my cabbages, and carrots with onions and leeks. I'll try adding lupins and foxgloves, which have a good reputation all over the garden, to my perennial beds, and more petunias here and there. I'll plant nasturtiums with broccoli and squash, spinach with strawberries, eggplants and beans together, and marigolds, as always, everywhere.

Blending in with nature, rather than fighting it, includes being aware of all aspects of the true essential nature of everything in the garden. Part of everything's true essential nature includes where it belongs and what companions belong with it. We don't have to be scientists to listen for the hints that nature gives us. This year, I learned about peppers and tomatoes. Who knows what I'll learn next year? I've heard that stinging nettles are good for adding iron to the soil; when I learn which plants need iron, I think weeding just might be a little bit easier.

NO EXPECTATIONS

The principal value of a private garden is not to give the possessor vegetable and fruit ... but to teach him patience and philosophy, and the higher virtues—hope deferred and expectations blighted.
                                        —Charles Dudley Warner

If your values are rigid, you can't really learn new facts. You've got to find some new clues, but before you can find them you've got to clear your head of old opinions. If you're plagued with value rigidity you can fail to see the answer even when it's staring you right in the face.

                                        —Robert M. Pirsig

The gardener can provide the frame, set up his easel, and sketch the pattern, but as time marches on he must constantly step aside and hand over his brush to Nature. This can be agony, to see all his cherished concepts being so drastically modified by Nature's ruthless fingers, but it can also be ecstasy.

                                        —Beverly Nichols

We start out each year with a million ideas and plans for our garden. We can't help but plant seeds and seedlings with some sort of visions of the flowers and fruits they will eventually produce. We do what we do, early in the year, because of these visions and plans. We lay the groundwork, literally, and arrange the raw materials in such a way as to create the garden of our visions, our dreams. We see masses of brilliant color, lush foliage, and abundant fruits and vegetables where only bare earth exists. The mind sees what the eye cannot.

In these early visions of what will happen in our garden, all of our flowers are beautiful, all of our vegetables are perfect and healthy. Everything comes up quickly and fills in completely. There are no plans made for vine-destroying grubs or hungry chipmunks; no dreams of yellow and brown withering leaves; no thoughts of disease, drought, insect infestation, or even garden-center mistakes. We expect every seed to sprout, every plant to blossom, every vine to be laden with waxy-looking fruits and veggies. Our garden will look just like the pictures in magazines.

This tendency toward perfectionism is hardly limited to gardening. We expect our bodies to do certain things in certain ways, to never fail us in any way; our choices and behaviors to have certain predictable consequences; and our relationships to proceed along specific, and of course pleasant, paths. When anything doesn't turn out exactly the way we expected, our response is often surprise, confusion, and anger. After all, that's the way it's *supposed* to be, right? We cling stubbornly and rigidly to our original views until forced to turn and see things in a new way.

In the garden, this perfectionism manifests itself very clearly. Our plants are supposed to take exactly as long as the seed packet says to germinate and mature; they should end up looking exactly like the picture on the little stick in the seedling pot; and they must be the biggest and best specimens in the neighborhood. Garden centers are expected to provide money-back guarantees and they probably grow a bit extra for this purpose; they *expect* some failures.

In my own garden this year, I have had to change many of my plans and give up many of my original expectations. I couldn't put my lilac bushes where I'd wanted to; all my pepper plants caught a virus and died; about half of my daylilies, clearly labeled "pink" by the garden center where I bought them, bore deep purple blossoms with yellow throats; and my zucchini plants produced lots of huge deep green leaves and big yellow flowers, and then suddenly collapsed, having provided plenty of food for the grubs and absolutely none for my family.

I have had to constantly adjust my thinking and change my expectations. Eventually, I began to realize that the only alternative to constant disappointment was to have no expectations at all. I continued tending my garden, but I tried to be completely open to whatever happened there. I thought of myself as flexible and able to adapt to anything nature might spring on me. I tried not to think of anything as a failure, but only a *change*. I tried to expect the unexpected, and then I had to learn not to even expect that. The Zen goal is no expectations or desires at all. While that in itself can become an impossible, perfectionist ideal, trying to attain it changes our perspective in a way that suddenly allows us to enjoy and appreciate *everything*.

Without intellectual judgments, things that happen just are; we can experience their reality without that dark cloud of dashed wishes and dreams.

We learn early in our culture to believe in right and wrong answers, good and bad outcomes. We learn to think in a logical, linear way: B follows A, C follows B; if this is true, then that must follow; if we do this, then that must result. So, when things happen that we didn't expect, it challenges our very method of thinking. It doesn't make sense to us; it isn't logical. Ironically, nature is always perfectly logical and correct; what we forget (or refuse to believe) is that *we don't know everything and we can't control everything.* These facts are not easy for human egos to accept. But accepting them is at the heart of learning to have no expectations, and having no expectations is at the heart of truly loving and enjoying our garden.

Everything in nature is happening exactly as it is supposed to happen; grubs are supposed to eat zucchini plants; aphids are supposed to eat tomatoes and carry viruses. Garden centers are not supposed to mislabel plants, but I even learned to accept that. The purple lilies are lovely. People are not perfect, and surprises aren't the end of the world. That's the lesson. We don't have to know every detail of everything going on in nature or anywhere else, and we couldn't do it if we tried. That's another lesson. We can't control anything outside of ourselves. That's probably the hardest lesson to learn.

Control is what all our plans and expectations are all about. If we can set everything up to have a certain and specific outcome, we are in control and we feel comfortable. If any factor in our plan takes off in a different direction, we lose control and feel scared. The illusion of control is the province of the human ego, and it serves us well in many areas of life. It also frequently ruins things for us. If we bring it into the garden, nature will quickly let us know who is in control—and it's not us. Then we have two choices: we can throw a tantrum and try, in vain, to regain control; or we can begin to let go and accept that things might just have a purpose and design that unfolds perfectly, beautifully, and to everyone's best advantage—when we let it.

Of course, I didn't like losing all my pepper and zucchini plants. Naturally, I was disappointed when some of my lilies bloomed in a different color than I'd expected. But then, I thought, *What difference does it really make?* Life in the garden is an exciting adventure. It's full of twists, turns, and surprises; it provides new information and lessons to learn. It's never, ever boring. Every year is totally new and different, every new garden patch a completely uncharted territory. Who knows what might happen there? And who really *wants* to know everything in advance? What fun would that be?

I've learned to take whatever happens in my garden in stride. The coleus in my deck planter didn't grow as large and full as I thought it would by now; an industrious little chipmunk seems to be sharing my crop of baby carrots; and my tomato plants have grown so incredibly large, I'm going to have to install a few eight-foot stakes to hold them up. All I can think about any of this is, *Isn't it all amazing?* When we step out of our human egos and just look at nature, we are awestruck. We can't help appreciating all of nature's twists and turns, the zig zag path of ultimate wisdom.

If we can learn to take the Zen attitude of *no expectations* in the garden, perhaps we can begin adopting it in other areas of life as well. When my car breaks down, it's not a disaster, it's just something that happens; when it turns out that I can't afford to do the work on my house I'd wanted to do this year, it's not the end of the world; when several of my coworkers resign at once, it's simply time for change. In truth, the time for surprise and change is *all the time*. Doesn't it keep life interesting?

MINDFULNESS

Whatever the tasks, do them slowly and with ease,
in mindfulness.
Don't do any task in order to get it over with.
Resolve to do each job in a relaxed way, with all
your attention.

—Thich Nhat Hanh

When you do something, you should do it with your
whole body and mind; you should be concentrated
on what you do.

— Shunryu Suzuki

The more fully we give our energy, the more it
returns to us.

—Jack Kornfield

This is happiness: to be dissolved into something
complete and great.

—Willa Cather

It is only when we enter into a moment and live it
with attention that we become truly alive.
                                        —Dorothy Gilman

A friend of mine told me this garden story: She was finally getting around to pulling down the dried and dead morning glory vines from the previous year. It wasn't something she *wanted* to do, but felt compelled by a little voice (that sounded very much like her mother's) in her mind admonishing her to get to it. She has a tendency to leave these kinds of chores until the last possible moment, spending her time in the garden on activities she finds more interesting and satisfying. But on this fine June day, she had decided to make herself get those dead vines cleared away.

The dried runners snaked their way up three seven-foot lengths of chicken wire nailed to the side of her garage. Some of the thicker vines were entwined together and quite strong. But the whole job looked like it shouldn't take more than fifteen minutes. Gloved and resolute, clippers in hand, she stepped into the flower bed with "Just do it!" running through her mind. She became a flurry of movement: clipping, pulling down, digging up and flinging out dead vines. All she thought about was that she had to get this done before she could go on to other more fun and interesting garden work. In the background of her driven busyness, she was vaguely aware of a pair of house finches nearby, flitting about and chirping loudly, but she paid no attention to them as she tugged at some of the tougher vines. She was getting closer and closer to being finished with this annoying chore that she had put off for so long.

She looked up to find the next catching point needing a judicious snip of the clippers and saw there, a foot above her head, the newly exposed cup-shaped nest she recognized as that of a house finch. Just as her eyes found it, the nest tilted forward and two small blue eggs tumbled out and fell to the ground, cracking open on a stepping stone. Suddenly she understood what the noisy finches had been trying to tell her. The eggs lay at her feet, destroyed. The nest hung above her head, empty. The two finches, now silent, perched for a moment longer in a nearby shrub, and then flew away.

My friend fought back the tears as she sank to the ground, filled with a painful sense of loss. Not only had she destroyed the eggs and disrupted the lives of a family of house finches who had chosen her garage for their nesting place, but she suddenly realized that she had closed herself off to the very reason she loves to garden: the connection with nature she feels when communing with the earth, greenery, and all the little creatures with whom she shares her small piece of land. Listening to the scolding voice in her mind, she had not heard the gentle voice of nature; intent on getting finished, she had not been aware of what she was doing when she was doing it.

This story illustrates the trap we so often fall into in gardening and so many other areas of life. We listen to the pushy, angry voices, the constant chatter in our minds, prattling on about the past and the future, and we completely miss the soft whispers of the here and now. Only when we act out of full awareness can we help, nurture, and create; whenever we act in nonawareness, the result is always destruction. Being aware in this way means not only knowing what our own hands are doing, but what effects are occurring far beyond us. Mindfulness means awareness not only of the pebble dropping into the water, but of all the ripples that follow.

Yesterday, I tied my tomato plants up to eight-foot stakes. They had outgrown their metal cages and were falling all over the place, laden down with abundant green fruit. I carefully lifted the long vines and leaned them against the wooden stakes, tying them there with soft flannel strips, so as not to bruise or cut their tender flesh. As I worked, I smelled the strong scent of tomato plants, basil, onions, garlic, and marigolds. I heard crows squawking from the tops of trees and dogs barking in the distance. I noticed the nearly transparent dragonflies hovering about.

From time to time, my mind would slip into its chatter mode, judging everything I was doing, filling me with concern about green tomatoes dropping off the vines as I worked and stakes breaking in two when I pushed them into the ground. I tried gently to bring my mind back into focus, to do everything very carefully, very gently, and very slowly. I closed my eyes and smelled the air, felt my breath, and came back to the present moment. I felt my hands as extensions of the tomato plants themselves. I lifted the vines and felt intuitively where they wanted to go. I left some of them unstaked, leaning here and there, wherever they seemed happiest. I gathered up the fallen fruit and put them in a paper bag to ripen.

Mindfulness means moving from a closed to an open state of mind, switching from a chattering mode to a silent, listening one. The tea ceremony is a classic practice of mindfulness. It is a meticulously performed ceremony of the usually simple acts of making and drinking tea. The point of it is to keep our minds totally focused, fully aware of each present moment. How many things do we do that way in our daily lives? We're usually running around, getting things done, over with, finished so that we can go on to the next thing. When are we fully concentrating on what is right here and right now?

Gardening offers us many opportunities to practice mindfulness. Weeding becomes a completely different experience when done this way: we can become fully aware of the movement of our hands, the feel of our fingertips as they touch the weeds and the soil, the tearing apart of the tiny roots underground as we pull, and the appearance and scent of every leaf and stem. Watering, planting, digging, raking, and picking fruits and vegetables can all be practiced mindfully, with our total attention and awareness. When our minds wander, as they are apt to do, we can simply bring them back by focusing on our breath for a moment. Then we can return our attention to the activities in which we are engaged. We can experience them as never before, with fresh new awareness.

My friend's story reminded me of the lesson of mindfulness. Now, whenever I am about to begin gardening, I take a moment to sit and breathe, to become fully aware of my body and everything around me. I spend a few minutes letting the garden tell me what to do, and then I do it slowly and carefully. When my mind wanders, I pause and ask myself what my fingers are feeling, what my ears are hearing, what scents I am smelling. Before my hands run off and do things I'll regret, I take the time to garden mindfully. And I love it more than ever.

THE KITCHEN GARDEN

If well-managed, nothing is more beautiful than the kitchen garden; the earliest blossoms come there: we shall in vain seek for flowering shrubs to equal the peaches, nectarines, apricots, and plums.

—William Cobbett

I have always thought a kitchen garden a more pleasant sight than the finest orangery. I love to see everything in perfection, and am more pleased to survey my rows of coleworts and cabbages, with a thousand nameless pot herbs springing up in their full fragrancy and verdue, than to see the tender plants of foreign countries.

—Joseph Addison

I came to love my rows, my beans, though so many more than I wanted. They attached me to the earth, and so I got strength like Antaeus.

—Henry David Thoreau

The things we grow in our flower gardens end up in various places: the compost heap, the trash, indoor vases and then the compost heap or trash. Their purpose is served in the garden itself, providing beauty in both image and scent. Then they are recycled into compost and serve the soil for another crop of plants, another season. But a kitchen garden is different. While looking and smelling as beautiful as any flower bed in the garden, the plants we grow there continue serving us in the capacity of beautiful, delicious, and nutritious food.

I've grown many kitchen gardens over the years, in many different places: city and country, backyard and window box. I've often had wonderful abundant results and sometimes fruitless vines that had to be pulled out of the garden halfway through the season. I've tried my hand at peppers, beans, spinach, eggplants, carrots, broccoli, cucumbers, lettuce, cabbage, Brussels sprouts, zucchini and other kinds of squash, onions, and garlic. I've spent hot August days canning tomatoes and pickling beets, and crisp October mornings picking pumpkins for pie.

I've always felt much more comfortable with vegetable plants than perennial flower beds. I suppose that has something to do with memories of my grandmother's garden. She always planted a few annuals, but veggies were clearly her strong suit. She grew the biggest, tastiest tomatoes and peppers I've ever found anywhere. She cared for and prepared her little garden plot lovingly, adding fresh peat moss and topsoil every year for thirty-some years. The soil was rich and black and scented with spearmint and basil. Runner beans climbed up a white trellis leaning against her garage; dandelions were cultivated as salad greens.

Until this year, I've always had pretty good luck with zucchini and peppers. I've never had any trouble growing beans, lettuces, cabbages, and broccoli; my cucumbers, climbing up trellises, have always been too abundant for my little family to eat them all ourselves. Root crops, such as beets and carrots, have been more dependent on good soil conditions and so have grown much better when I planted them in the country than in my city gardens. Melons require a longer growing season than anyplace I have lived, although other people seem to have managed to grow them locally. I've never grown sweet corn, because I haven't had the space in the city and when I lived in the country it seemed silly, surrounded as I was by cornfields. Whatever I haven't grown myself, I have hunted at farmers' markets every summer.

Of all the vegetables I've grown over the years, one stands out as my particular favorite as well as the one I've always been able to grow extremely well: tomatoes. I've grown big boys, early girls, plum roma, beefsteak, cherry, and patio varieties. I've grown them in small backyards, big backyards, pots on decks, and window boxes outside urban apartments. They have never been anything but abundant, beautiful, and delicious for me. They like to be surrounded by basil and parsley, and I have been happy to accommodate them; I pick all three together to dice into pasta sauces and rice dishes.

The tomato's natural enemies are aphids, hornworms, and cutworms. Nematodes can also attack the plants' roots. I always grow lots of marigolds around my tomatoes; they are the best controllers of nematodes in the garden and also help with the insects. Its important to plant marigolds early and let them take root; their effects on the soil also carry over from one year to the next. Nasturtiums are great aphid traps and ladybugs also feed on these pests naturally (you can actually buy ladybugs for this purpose). I've found natural, organic sprays—made mostly of ground-up red peppers or onions and garlic—to be very effective insect repellents. I snap off lower shoots and suckers to aid the growth of the main stems. Staking keeps the fruit off the ground (where worms live) and helps the stems bear their weight. Good soil and drainage (and luck) have always kept my tomatoes disease-free.

Sometimes green tomatoes fall off the vine, and while many people cook with them as they are, I place them in paper bags to ripen. Keeping them away from sunlight allows them to turn red without rotting: on the vine they need sun, off the vine they need darkness. Once they turn red, I use them immediately before they rot. Refrigeration or freezing turns them icy (then mushy when thawed) and tasteless. If your crop is anything like mine, you'll need to can some of your tomatoes for future use. This is done using a boiling-bath method and clean glass canning jars. Sometimes I can them alone, with a bit of salt; other times I add chopped onions and peppers. Either way, they are wonderful, delicious reminders of your summer garden on cold winter days. If you're used to store-bought tomatoes, you won't believe the flavorful difference in these home-grown gems, fresh or canned.

If space is limited, grow patio varieties in pots or window boxes. Cherry tomatoes aren't necessarily a good choice, unless they are specifically a patio variety. Just because the tomatoes are small, doesn't mean that the plants will be; my cherry tomato plants are some of the largest in my garden. If you have more room, there are all kinds of tomatoes to choose from. Roma or plum tomatoes are the Italian variety, used for pasta sauces. They are meatier and less watery than other, larger varieties. Beefsteak will be your largest type of fruit, full of juice and seeds. Big boys and early girls produce flavorful medium-sized tomatoes. Cherry tomatoes are big producers of fruit that can range from one-half inch to over an inch in diameter. They are wonderful added to green salads or just sliced in half and tossed with basil, parsley, or other fresh herbs. Red wine vinegar and olive oil with a hint of garlic can be added for a complete cherry tomato salad.

Notice the maturation periods on your tomato varieties, as there is a wide range of differences between them. I like to grow both early and later-maturing types so that I have fruit ripening throughout a longer period of time. Nonetheless, I always have a lot of tomatoes ready for picking at once. That's why I learned how to can them. Canning is a good way to preserve many of your kitchen garden products, either plain or pickled. Combinations of veggies can also make great relishes and jams. One of my favorites is a recipe of my grandmother's made with different kinds of peppers preserved in olive oil.

I've never been fortunate enough to have my own orchard of fruit trees or even a stand of bramble fruits (raspberries and blackberries) or blueberry bushes. I've tried growing strawberries, but found the little animals in my garden too greedy to share their harvest with me. So I have contented myself with haunting farmers' markets for red and black raspberries, strawberries, apples, peaches, pears, and plums. I've made fabulous peach and strawberry preserves, and an almost infinite variety of apple dishes, including apple butter that takes days to cook and gives new meaning to the phrase, "melts in your mouth." Blueberry pies and pancakes never last long in my house, and pears canned with a touch of food coloring have graced many of our holiday tables. If you live someplace where you can grow fruit, my advice is that you do it in abundance. Fruit and fruit desserts are to a meal what flowers are to a garden: pure beauty in an otherwise practical and nourishing landscape.

Both veggies and fruit can be eaten fresh from the garden as snacks, and since this is the way most of us eat now, this is an important element in the value of our kitchen garden. Keeping our pest control methods organic helps keep the produce edible without having to be scrubbed, peeled, and cooked. While we always need to wash our fruits and veggies before eating them, the less they are cooked, the more natural flavor and nutrients they retain. Freeing ourselves from a lot of preparation, we can munch on fresh carrots, tomatoes, green beans, lettuce, onions, peppers, zucchini, and cucumbers straight from the garden, feeding both body and soul.

The taste and scent of fresh veggies and fruits reminds us of our closeness to the earth. We feel more connected to nature when our food comes right out of the ground before our very eyes. We recognize the ability of the planet to nourish us. Raising our own food keeps us more closely connected to its source. The fewer middlemen there are between us and the earth, the more we can see and appreciate our relationship to it. Our relationship with our garden becomes more real, more personal, more intimate when it brings more than just pretty flowers into our homes and lives. The kitchen garden brings us life itself. While we are one with all the plants in our gardens, metaphorically and spiritually, we become one with the food from our gardens *literally*. The produce of our kitchen garden ends up in us, a true part of our bodies and selves. The earth enters into us, giving life and nourishment. We are one with the vegetables, the garden, and the earth, all drinking from and swimming together in the ocean of life.

WEATHER

There is a sumptuous variety about the New England weather that compels the stranger's admiration—and regret. The weather is always doing something there; always attending strictly to business. But it gets through more business in spring than in any other season. In the spring I have counted one hundred and thirty-six different kinds of weather inside of twenty-four hours.

—Mark Twain

A good gardener always plants three seeds—one for the grubs, one for the weather, and one for himself.

—C. Collins

The spring started off with a bang this year. Weatherwise, that is. Early in April, a wild windstorm swept through, tearing the awnings off our house and knocking down our back fence. The wind blew gustily for hours, howling fiercely as it attempted to destroy everything in its path. I marveled that, though they swayed back and forth with the wind, none of my big old trees dropped any larger branches (later in the season, though, I wondered if the storm had weakened them enough to fall at another time). It made me think about the natural sway architects build into skyscrapers to keep them from falling over or at least losing lots of windows every time it storms.

After that, the spring came late, almost unwillingly, to this area. The late spring took its toll on my garden. At least I blamed the late spring for the perennial ground covers that didn't come back this year, the browning evergreen shrubs, and the uncharacteristically feeble-looking hosta plants. The warm temperatures came late and then departed again for a week of chilly rain. May felt like April and June felt like May.

This was then followed by a hot, humid, and wet summer. Records were broken for the most days over 90 degrees, and 100 was reached earlier and more often than ever before. News of dying cattle and house pets spread quickly throughout the midwest. Several hundred people died as a result of the heat in Chicago. The humidity was unbearable. I could tell when it went down, because my windows would open higher and more easily when they weren't swollen with the moisture thickening the air.

I would have thought that my plants would love such warmth and humidity. Isn't that what greenhouses and conservatories always feel like? But they looked as wilted and worn out from the weather as the rest of us. We watered them often, and they made a valiant effort to recover, but all the strangeness of this year's weather took its toll. They just aren't quite as cheerful and bright and strong as usual. Some of them didn't bother coming up at all this year, or came up and then quickly faded rather than spreading and growing.

While hurricanes pound the beaches in other parts of the country, in the midwest we become accustomed to tornado warnings and flood watches. The potholes winter leaves behind in our streets fill with water and we shake our heads and exclaim to one another, "Oh well, at least it's not a blizzard!" We like to think of ourselves as tough here, when it comes to weather. No snow, sleet, or cold temperatures keep us from our ice hockey, ice fishing, figure skating, cross-country skiing, or just walking and running outdoors. We get ourselves to work on days when cities in other parts of the country would shut down completely. A little old summer storm is nothing to us. We're more interested in capturing dramatic video film of a tornado touchdown than in seeking shelter from it.

But our gardens take a beating from all this exciting weather. In the few short months they have to grow, they must withstand torrential rains and resulting floods, lightning strikes, windstorms, high temperatures, and unbelievable humidity. While we escape into our air-conditioned buildings and cars (we're much braver against cold than heat), our poor gardens suffer whatever nature dishes out. My delicate impatiens shrivel and shrink; my little Johnny-jump-ups get matted to the ground; my coleus grows sporadically, and some of it not at all; my carrot and lettuce seeds all wash down to one end of their raised bed and grow in clumps rather than rows.

Battered and bruised, the plants in our gardens pick themselves up and try again and again. The life force in them is strong; they take whatever good they can from everything that happens and make the best of it. Sometimes farmers lose portions of their crops due to the weather, and so they always grow extra in anticipation of the unexpected drought, flood, or storm damage. In our own gardens, we can do the same thing, up to a point. Sometimes we just have to give up on a whole crop of vegetables or bed of flowers when nature is too harsh.

My garden seems confused by this year's weather. Everything is trying hard, but with the exception of my indestructible tomato plants and some extraordinarily hardy annuals, things are showing some effects from the unusual spring and summer weather. But then, I don't remember a year when people went around saying, "Isn't this *usual* weather we're having?" There's always something unusual about the weather: temperature, rainfall, humidity, or storms. One winter a few years back, we had hardly any snow here, and the spring thaw was correspondingly dry. This affected the plant life around here all summer.

A few years ago, my house and a tree nearby were hit by lightning; the house has been repaired, but now the tree has to be cut down. The weather is always with us and can sometimes affect us for a long time to come. It's one of the earth's features we can't control and must adapt to. As I watch television coverage of another hurricane heading for the eastern United States, I can't help wondering about all those people who built all those houses right there on the ocean, knowing their property could disappear overnight in one of these storms. But then, I plant my garden year after year, knowing that I may lose some or all of it to acts of nature. Some perennials may not winter over; a flash flood could wipe out all my vegetable plants; strong winds could throw tree branches, patio furniture, or fencing around, causing irreparable damage to my garden.

We battle the elements because they're there, and we have to take our chances with them. Sometimes they're kind, other times they seem harsh. But they're always doing exactly what they're supposed to do. The weather's true unpredictability adds excitement to our gardening life. Its occasional surprises and changes keep our attention, lest we drift off into mindless complacency. It provides our gardens with sunshine, water, and warmth; keeps them alive and growing; and keeps us alive along with them.

In this part of the country, summer is a welcome though brief respite between cold, harsh winters. The warmer temperatures give us a chance to relax for a bit before bracing for the next bout of freezing weather. Therefore, we try to make the most of summers here. We grow whatever we can in the short season in which anything will grow. Inclement summer weather just doesn't seem so bad when the rest of the year brings blizzards and subfreezing temperatures. Only lightning strikes will get us off the golf course; nothing keeps us out of the garden.

I don't like to spend a lot of time outdoors when it's freezing in the winter, but I do go out and do everything I need to do and I feel the cold. In the summer, I go outdoors whether it's wet, hot, or humid. I feel the rain on my skin, breathe the hot or cool air, take in the sunshine and cloudiness. I know these elements because I have actually experienced them firsthand. I continue experiencing them because I don't want to forget what they are, what it feels like to be one with them. I don't want to experience life without weather. Whatever it does to or for my garden, it is a very basic part of nature, just like my plants and soil and animals—and me. We are all part of one natural world, whole and indivisible.

SEEING

*As you walk down the street you can tune your
"receiver" into the world on any number of channels.
Each way of tuning creates a different street. But the
street doesn't change. You do.*

—Ram Dass

*Of all the people who have passed by your yard,
how many have really seen the almond tree?*

—Thich Nhat Hanh

*To see a world in a grain of sand
And Heaven in a wild flower,
Hold infinity in the palm of your hand
And eternity in an hour.*

—William Blake

*While with an eye made quiet by the power,
Of harmony and the deep power of joy,
We see into the life of things.*

—William Wordsworth

Perception is one of the trickiest parts of being human. Most of the time, we don't see what is right in front of us and we do see all kinds of things that aren't there at all. Seeing doesn't really happen in our eyes; it happens in our mind, and all kinds of other memories, beliefs, and viewpoints are thrust upon whatever we're looking at. Different people viewing the same thing report completely different descriptions of it.

It is often said that we only see what we want to see, but that's too simplistic. We see a lot of things we don't wish to, but yet *choose* to see. The issue of choice is what makes perception so confused and difficult for us. We choose the *meanings* that we give to everything we see. It's not that we only see what we want to see, but that we only see what our eyes and minds are *open* to seeing. Most of the time, they aren't very open at all. We choose narrow little perceptions based on what we expect, what we already believe, and what we think we're *supposed* to see.

We narrow our focus to one angle or perspective: scientific, artistic, academic, emotional, political, and so on. We choose these different perceptions based on our position or job in a given situation, but we also carry this selective seeing into all areas of life. We see what isn't there; we don't see what is there. We ignore whatever doesn't fit into our preconceived notions or whatever we have determined to be inconsequential. We invent whatever we expect to find, even if it isn't there. Essentially, what we end up seeing wherever we look is a rather accurate reflection of ourselves.

In the garden, we project all of our expectations, fears, doubts, education, beliefs, and prejudices onto innocent nature. We constantly judge and compare everything instead of just looking and seeing it as it really is. We put our perceptions onto what we see rather than letting it reveal itself to us. Our garden exists as much in our minds as in the physical world.

If we are free to choose our perceptions and viewpoints, then what is the Zen viewpoint? Basically, it is no viewpoint. It is *just seeing*—like just sitting, just walking, or just gardening. It is complete openness, beginner's mind, or receptiveness. It is letting ourselves be told what is in front of us; allowing everything to reveal itself in its own way and time. In the garden, it means simply *looking*, with open eyes and minds and hearts. The delicate yellow bloom, the sturdy green stalk, the shiny red fruit all have their stories to tell. The yellowing leaves can tell us to stop watering them so much, the wilted leaves to water them more. The stunted growth of marigolds in the shade or impatiens in bright sunshine can show us our mistakes.

Sometimes what our plants have to tell us is even simpler: beauty, life, birth, growth, death, drought, juiciness. Sometimes, if we're really open to them, they reveal the secrets of life and the universe. There are no words for these secrets; we can only discover them by just looking and just seeing. The garden is a magical, holy place, where everything in nature can be revealed to us, and everything in ourselves and our lives and the world as well.

It's hard to write about this *just seeing* because it's something you *just do*. Choose one plant and just sit with it for a while. Look at it, up close. Try to turn off the chatter in your mind and receive messages instead of sending them out. When the volume gets turned up again on that insistent, perpetual inner monologue, simply let it go and gently return your full attention to just seeing what's in front of you. It's like in meditation, when you return your focus to your breath in order to regain peace. Do this same exercise with many small plants, flowers, leaves, or vegetables in your garden. Do it with the garden as a whole or with one portion of it at a time. Simply empty out and let it fill you up.

When you spend a few minutes being truly open (and that's about as long as most of us can do it) to just seeing, we bring back something new to our daily perceptions. Once you have just stared at a plant while trying to empty your mind and let that plant show itself to you, you can never look at it in quite the same way. Then you start looking at other plants with new eyes. And then your eyes begin to open at other times, in other places, looking at other things. Before you know it, your perceptions have changed. You are able to see more than you ever could before.

It's a gift of our gardens that they can teach us how to just see. It's a wonderful side effect of gardening that we can experience this new perceptiveness. Less interpreting and investing things with meaning and more just looking at them receptively can change our whole outlook. We can see all situations and people with new eyes; we can recognize what is truly in front of us rather than projecting what is already in our minds out there, like holograms. It's not that suddenly we don't see anything negative and only see the positive, it's that *we see reality better*. All we have to do is *just see*, without the cloudy glasses of our old perceptions. And we can begin in the garden.

I watched a bee on a sunflower for a few minutes the other day. Afterward, I walked and worked in the garden without my usual alertness for and fear of bees. I don't know why or how it happened, but after staring at that furry little insect, frantically performing its instinctive work in nature, I just didn't automatically recoil when I heard that familiar buzzing sound. One day I focused on my rosemary bush, a plant I usually concentrate on smelling rather than seeing: its tiny leaves, almost like pine needles, must be positively filled with oil to give off such a strong and wonderful scent. Last week, a green tomato on the vine captured my full attention: the little bulb sat silently drinking away at the nourishment running through the vine, slowly pumping itself up like a balloon until it couldn't hold anymore; then it would begin developing that rich tomato flavor and color. Today I'm going to spend some time just looking at my first deep purple eggplant, a vegetable I have never grown before. Who knows what I might see?

COMMUNICATION

Shall I not have intelligence with the earth? Am I not partly leaves and vegetable mould myself?
—Henry David Thoreau

As I work among my flowers, I find myself talking to them, reasoning and remonstrating with them, and adoring them as if they were human beings.
—Celia Thaxter

Speak to the earth and it will teach thee.

—Job 12:8

To get the best results you must talk to your vegetables.

—Prince Charles

I had to leave town for a few days in the spring. It was an inconvenient time to leave as far as the garden was concerned. I had just begun digging and building, planning and planting. Before I left, I walked through my garden, telling the plants, trees, and bushes that

I'd be gone for a few days. I didn't want them to feel neglected or abandoned. I knew it was the busy season, time to be digging and planting and building and fertilizing and all of that. But it couldn't be helped. I had to go. I told my garden that when I came back, I would have my daughter with me, and they would love her. She has a way with animals and children and plants; they all love her.

When I got back, I went right out and told them I was home. I asked them how they'd been doing, and I could see that they were fine. Nothing had happened to them, no bad weather or anything; they hadn't wilted or shriveled or died in my absence. I introduced them all to my daughter, and as she walked through the garden, I could see that they loved her.

Throughout the season, I have spoken to my garden, telling it how well it looks, asking if there are some things I should do for it. I never criticize anything, but if it looks like there are some problems, I ask about them. I tell the plants what I'm doing when I thin, pick, fertilize, water, or plant something new in their midst. Sometimes I talk about other things: the weather, the day I'm having, my writing, my troubles. In the garden, I praise, admire, vent, and commune. I practice my relationship with the plant life there. I tell the plants how I feel. My garden is a wonderful nonjudgmental listener. We all need that.

Does a garden really know what we're feeling? Do we garden differently when we're happy, sad, angry, or tired? When we're feeling incompetent in the garden or unsure of ourselves? Do the plants pick up on these things? Did they really know I was gone or what I was saying to them before and after my trip? If we accept that *commu-*

nication and *speech* are two different things, then how can we not
believe that at least the feelings underlying our words are conveyed
to the living beings we work with in the garden? Not everything is
communicated or understood through ears.

My grandmother used to praise her plants when they grew strong
and healthy. She thanked them for their beautiful fruits and vegetables
when she picked them. She also scolded them when they strayed
where they didn't belong. She asked them what was the matter when
they drooped or didn't produce much fruit or flowers. She touched
them lovingly, brushing her hand across their tops, like tousling a
child's hair. No garden I have ever seen grew so strong and healthy
and beautiful or produced more delicious food and flowers.

Communication between humans can be so very confused and
difficult that often we escape to the garden, where we feel less mis-
understood. The garden is a wonderful place to practice our communication skills, particularly those that are nonverbal. Call it vibes
or energy or whatever, the plants in our care do respond to what we
send out while we're working with them, touching them, or just looking them over. They do respond differently to music or angry voices,
singing or silence. The feelings we impart to them become as much a
part of them as the water and sunshine they take in.

I've hung a wind chime in my garden, and its soft, melodic voice
soothes me while I'm working there. I put a radio/tape player on the
kitchen window sill, and play Mozart for the garden. I hum while I
work. My garden hears all kinds of other sounds as well: birds and
squirrels, leaves rustling in the trees overhead, dogs and people in the
neighborhood. Outside the fence, cars drive by, and the sounds of

people on rollerblades and kids on bicycles fill the air. Noisy garbage trucks take over the alleys once a week, and road repair crews visit occasionally. My garden hears a full range of city life going on all around it. How different its aural life would be somewhere else—in a suburban cul-de-sac or out in the country.

I believe my garden takes in all of these sounds, including my voice and the pleasant sounds I deliberately provide for it. But is this a one-way conversation? Does my garden communicate back to me? I think so. I think it expresses itself in its color and form, its scents and flavors. I think it responds to me, and everything around it, through its growth and decay, its wilting and its flourishing. I think the garden is exquisitely eloquent. It tells me when it's happy or not so happy, when it needs something it isn't getting, when it's feeling young and jubilant or old and tired.

A garden responds to the love it is given, the care and attention it receives from human hands. In addition to good soil, proper nourishment, water, and sunlight, a garden needs our love. Since it is not growing wild, away from human influence, on its own with the rest of the natural world, our relationship with it is an important factor in its health and happiness. When we take care to express our pleasure in it, our love for it, and our desire to provide it with everything it needs to grow and thrive, it *knows*. When we treat it as if we don't care, or don't expect it to do well, it won't.

I knew someone once who always felt that she couldn't garden, that only people with a special gift in that area—a green thumb—could grow plants, and other people shouldn't even try. Well, at least *she* shouldn't try. Her strong feelings of inadequacy in the garden came from having a mother who was so brilliant in the garden, she felt she couldn't compete with her and couldn't face the possibility of failure. Her few attempts to grow anything at all resulted in weak, feeble specimens that barely lived. Her constant exclamations that "I can't grow anything; my mother's the gardener in our family" may have had something to do with it.

What is the difference between a person with a green thumb and everyone else? Contrary to what many of us believe, it is not necessarily education in the area of horticulture or a talent one is born with. It is open, loving communication with nature that makes a person able to grow a garden. It's letting go of fear, doubt, worry, and trying to do things perfectly; it's trusting in nature and recognizing oneself as a part of it, along with the plants, animals, soil, air, rain, and sunlight. Having a green thumb means getting in there and becoming one with the earth. Anyone can do it, because we're all human, all part of nature's harmonious plan, all truly one with all other expressions of the life force.

If you're one of those people who is convinced that you just don't have a green thumb, try this: tell your plants about your doubts and fears. Talk to them about not knowing exactly what to do for them to help them grow and flourish happily. Tell them you're willing to try this gardening thing, but you need them to help you, to show you what they need from you. Relax and try to be open to hearing their answers. Try to let go of the belief that you either do or don't know what you're doing in the garden—you don't have to know. Trust nature. Become one with it. Let it tell you what to do. Accept its twists and turns, its failures and surprises. Don't take anything to heart except the joy and pleasure of working with the earth, *playing* with it, talking and listening to it. Remember that your goal is not having a picture of your garden in some glossy magazine but simply having a wonderful time communing with nature. Flowers and vegetables, if they come, are just an added bonus.

Some people like to personify the energy of their gardens by imagining garden angels or fairies. This is great if it helps you to communicate with nature. But the Zen of gardening is realizing your true oneness with the earth and all of its expressions of life. You are your garden's angel, the being capable of nurturing and assisting the magical, miraculous nature of everything in it. The magic is in you and in the soil, plants, insects, birds, animals, air, and sunlight. When all of these elements begin communicating openly with one another, who knows what miracles might result?

FINDING PEACE

When the world wearies, and society ceases to satisfy, there is always the garden.

—Minnie Aumonier

Nature's peace will flow into you as sunshine flows into trees. The winds will blow their own freshness into you, and the storms their energy, while cares will drop off like autumn leaves.

—John Muir

Perhaps the reason for this love of nonhuman nature is that communion with it restores to us a level of our own human nature at which we are still sane, free from humbug, and untouched by anxieties.

—Alan W. Watts

*All my hurts
My garden spade can heal.*

—Ralph Waldo Emerson

I don't know how people deal with their moods
when they have no garden, raspberry patch or field to
work in. You can take your angers, frustrations,
bewilderments to the earth, working savagely,
working up a sweat and an ache and a great
weariness. The work rinses out the cup of your spirit,
leaves it washed and clean and ready to be freshly
filled with new hope.

—Rachel Peden

Working in the garden, I try to bring my best, highest, most positive energy. I want to impart my joy and love to the things growing there. I want to have the best possible effect I can on my garden. But sometimes, being human, I don't feel quite up to being happy and positive. Sometimes I feel angry or sad, or just crabby or out of sorts. We humans have our moods. Things happen to and around us that cause us to feel all kinds of things, from annoyance to rage, disappointment to shock. While practicing Zen tends to keep our responses to life on the lower end of that reactionary scale, we still feel things and not all of those things are particularly pleasant.

I have found myself in a quandary this year, wondering whether I should go into the garden when I'm in one of these kinds of moods. Should I protect my garden from my negative thoughts and feelings? Should I stay away from my sensitive plants when all I really want to do is vent anger or wallow in sorrow? Or should I adopt a false cheerfulness and go about my gardening pretending that everything is all right? If I do that, will my garden be fooled or will it be able to sense the discrepancy between my false front and my true energy?

Again, I found myself thinking of my garden as my child. While children do need protection from many of the issues and problems adults must deal with, they also know when anyone is not feeling well. They respond with one of their sweet gentle kisses, and pat you with their tiny hands. They are sympathetic by nature, telling you that you will feel better soon. And, instantly, you do. How can you help but feel better, faced with their open, honest concern and love? It is our job, as adults, to give children all that we can that is good for them, but sometimes they also have a great deal to give to us. Our relationships with our gardens can be very much the same.

When you least feel like it, gardening can be the best thing you can do. Recently, I advised a friend who was overworked, underappreciated, and stressed out to force himself out into his garden daily. I don't think he took my advice, but when I'd heard that he was relieved of his position for complaining about it, I took my own outrage to the garden. Digging dirt and pulling weeds, I felt myself travel through a range of emotional responses to what had happened.

How could people in positions of power make decisions that affect other people's lives based on so little information, and be so short-sighted and callous? I ripped out delicate clover weeds viciously and tossed them aside. *Why did it seem that there were always people just waiting for an opening to get what they wanted, regardless of who they had to trample over to get it?* I attacked the soil savagely with my hoe. *Was it true, after all, that nice guys always do finish last?* I felt my anger turn to sadness. *Was I simply foolish to have so much faith in the ultimate goodness of humankind?* I closed my eyes and breathed in rosemary-scented air. *Where were all these morals and values people were always talking about?* I picked green beans for dinner and flowers to fill a vase. Gradually, my mind stopped talking to itself. In the silence, I recognized the smallness of human choices within the larger scheme of things; the pettiness of people in relation to the immense natural world within which we live; the truth of the law of karma and the inevitability of restored balance. Everything happens for a reason; every moment is perfect, exactly as it is. Everything will be all right.

I go into my garden, however I'm feeling, and make myself engage it in conversation. Sometimes I work hard, burning off emotions that need vigorous expression. Other times, I just sit and look and listen or meditate on the bare ground under a tree. My garden doesn't seem to mind my negative emotions, but magically eases them. I always leave my garden feeling better than I did when I entered it. No matter how large or small our problems are, the garden can always help.

Gardening makes us feel good because it brings us in direct contact with the earth and our own true essential nature. So much of what we spend our time and energy on is political and unnatural; the garden can be a welcome oasis that heals us at our deepest level. It refreshes and restores us to our true selves. It gives us the strength to go back out there and face all of our tasks, issues, and problems with renewed energy. It gives us peace, and there is nothing in life that peace does not improve.

When we're feeling upset, we've lost sight of the basic truths of the universe. We think something should be other than what it is. We want something that isn't. We don't want something that is. When we have found peace in our gardens, we return to find that nothing in our lives or the world has changed—except us. Everything looks different through peaceful eyes. The peace inside us is projected onto everything we see. While there is still injustice and suffering in the world, we discover a way of fighting it by redirecting its energy—the very same energy that runs through all of us and through everything in the universe—rather than becoming a brick wall that will be knocked down by it.

In tai chi, we use very slow, deliberate body movements to learn to focus our attention and feel the energy of the universe. It is a practice, like meditating or performing the tea ceremony, that brings us back to the present moment, the here and now. We learn the calm concentration that puts us in touch with our natural inner peace. The energy that extends from that deep, inner peace follows its natural flow through us and out into the world. With calm focus and concentration, we stop blocking that flow of energy. This is not a forcing or creating of anything new, but rather a new recognition of what is eternally true and natural.

When we approach gardening with this kind of focus and calm, our work becomes Zen practice that flows smoothly and peacefully. But when we go into the garden with all of our human feelings, when we bring the garden all of our troubles, the garden miraculously brings us back to our true selves, our natural peaceful state. It becomes a different kind of Zen practice. Through our interactions with it, the garden gives us the gift of peace. We leave our worry, sorrow, and anger on its altar and are cleansed.

I no longer ask myself whether or not I should go into the garden at any time, feeling or thinking anything. It is always time to go into the garden. I always find peace there, no matter what is going on in my life or in my self. The peaceful energy of the universe flows through the earth and all of my plants and into me. I find peace in the eye of a sunflower, the root of a carrot, the scent of rosemary. I find peace in digging soil, planting seeds, and stirring compost. I find peace in breathing the same air as my maple trees and tomato vines. Peace dwells in the true nature of all nature, in everything that lives in my garden. Whenever I need it, it is there to heal and nourish me, body and soul.

PURE PLEASURE

Gardening gives me fun and health and knowledge. It gives me laughter and colour. It gives me pictures of almost incredible beauty.

—John F. Kenyon

To dig one's own spade into one's own earth! Has life anything better to offer than this?

—Beverly Nichols

He who plants a garden, plants happiness.

—Chinese proverb

A morning glory at my window satisfies me more than the metaphysics of books.

—Walt Whitman

There is more pleasure in making a garden than in contemplating a paradise.

—Anne Scott-James

No occupation is so delightful to me as the culture of
the earth . . . and no culture comparable to that of
the garden.
                                                    —Thomas Jefferson

And forget not that the earth delights to feel your
bare feet and the wind longs to play with your hair.
                                                    —Kahlil Gibran

The joys of gardening are hard to describe to anyone who hasn't
known firsthand the ache of muscles that have turned over a plot of
soil; the scent of basil, mint, rosemary, and marigolds on their hands;
the sight of seedlings bursting from the ground and fruit ripening on
their own vines. And yet those who have succumbed to nature's se-
duction are so many and so varied in every way, that this joy can be
called universal. It is a possibility inherent in being human. If we heed
the call and venture out there into the world of gardening, we all find
the same peace and joy in our communion with nature.

The ancient Chinese, Middle Eastern, Western European, and
Early American gardeners who took pen in hand to express the pure
pleasure of roots, flowers, soil, and vegetables all tell the same story.
Today, as never before, we need to reconnect with nature, to return
to the Garden of Eden and reclaim our place in the natural world.
We need the refreshment of body and the renewal of spirit that gardening offers. If for no other reason—if not for food or property
values or medicine or visual appeal—we need our gardens simply for
the opportunity to perform the act of gardening.

Earlier this season, I found myself feeling somewhat guilty for spending so much time and energy (and money) on my garden. I enjoyed it so much that it felt like something I shouldn't be doing. My world seemed to get very small as I focused my attention on getting my garden off to a good start for the year. Something in me actually felt selfish for feeling so good about my own little garden. Something that was so pleasurable, so delightful, so much fun had to be bad. People out there in the world were starving, fighting, killing one another, stealing from the disadvantaged, and battling disease. Who was I to bring so much of my attention to so frivolous a pursuit as backyard gardening? I didn't know exactly what I should be doing instead, but little pangs of guilt kept surfacing in my consciousness, belittling my efforts.

In her lovely little book, *Now Zen*, author Joko Beck writes, "There is a lot of arrogance in guilt." Why would I feel guilty unless I had some grandiose notion of being in control of the whole world? Why would I second-guess where I was and what I was doing unless I thought I could or should be doing something better? Why was I judging my present moment so harshly instead of enjoying it as a gift? Why did I presume to think that gardening wasn't a good enough way to spend my time and energy? There was indeed a lot of arrogance in my guilt.

In our Western culture, we have been well-trained to believe that anything pleasurable is something we shouldn't be doing, at least not until all our work is done. Since we define work as whatever we don't want to do, all the work in gardening doesn't feel like work—it's not painful enough. We enjoy it, we love it, it feels great, so it must be bad, or at least small and insignificant, something people do when they have nothing else to do.

Gradually, I got over my guilt about gardening as I learned to accept the pleasure it gave me. I began to feel less and less as if I had any choice about whether or not to garden. It was there, I was there; we interacted, sharing our present moments. The Zen attitude is acceptance and nonjudgment, nonresistance, and noninterference with the natural flow of energy and essential reality of everything. Sometimes it's even harder for us to let go and accept what is nice, pleasant, and abundant than what is difficult or painful. But there is as much human arrogance in rejecting pleasure as there is in resisting suffering. Nature consists of both.

Working the little bit of nature in my care is as good a way to expend my time and energy as anything else. Any activity at all, done in mindfulness and care, in acceptance and peace, can be Zen practice. It is only our human ego that judges and ranks one activity over another. When we keep our minds peaceful, open, and accepting, the right things to do present themselves to us. When we do them mindfully, attentively, carefully, and slowly, respecting their essential nature and our own, they are elevated. Scrubbing a floor, making tea, raking a bed of stones into a serene pattern, or cultivating roses can all be equally perfect Zen moments. It is not what we do, it is how we do it. If pleasure is part of the essential nature of an activity, then pleasure is part of doing that activity mindfully. The feel of a warm, gentle breeze against my skin, the sound of cicadas humming above me, the scent of herbs and flowers, the sight of beautiful colors on leaves and petals, the taste of a red cherry tomato bursting in my mouth—it is part of my essential nature to find pleasure in these things.

I think we get confused about what is our essential nature and what is our superficial, human ego nature. We call things like greed, violence, and self-importance "human nature." But these are only the expressions of our topmost layer, our outer shell as human beings. We must go many levels beneath that to find our true essential nature, the true reality of humanness. We find it in mindful practice, in carefully focused attention, and in silence. We find it quietly waiting for us in those moments when the endless chattering of our conscious minds becomes still. We find it in the joyful practice of gardening.

I can no longer think of gardening as anything other than pure pleasure, even when it's hard work or doesn't produce perfect results (according to my ego's judgmental standards). It feels wonderful no matter how it goes or what it does or does not produce. It touches me on all levels, filling my body, mind, and soul with joy. It takes me out of my small human self and brings me home to my real, true essential nature. Gardening is a trip around the world and throughout the entire universe, all without leaving my own backyard. And the trip is pure pleasure.

SITTING

W*hen you sit, just sit.*

—Yun-man

I am spending delightful afternoons in my garden, watching everything living around me. As I grow older, I feel everything departing, and I love everything with more passion.

—Emile Zola

Zen Buddhists talk about "just sitting," a meditative practice in which the idea of duality of self and object does not dominate one's consciousness.

—Robert M. Pirsig

When I walk in my garden, I speak to it, listen to it, touch it, and look closely at it; when I sit in my garden, I *just sit*. Sometimes I meditate, other times I just sit there, observing everything around me and observing myself observing everything around me. Sometimes I sit in the garden to have a good think, to examine an issue, or make an important decision. Other times, I try to empty my mind of all thoughts.

I first learned how to meditate twenty-five years ago. My teacher at the time taught me to meditate in a very simple way, with physical relaxation, counting, and breathing very slowly. I practiced trying to empty my mind, which was not easy, with millions of thoughts racing around in there at breakneck speed. But just becoming aware of them helped me to move into a deeper state of meditation. I was at least able to slow down the stream of thoughts endlessly chattering in my head. I focused on a simple image, like a white wall, and let the chatter drift away. I let go of feelings, worries, words, and pictures, past and future, and relaxed into a state of suspended thought, a kind of wakeful sleep. It was like nothing I had ever experienced before.

After only a week or two of meditating for fifteen minutes or so twice a day, I felt profound changes in myself and my daily life. Situations, people, and events that had bothered me before suddenly elicited absolutely no reaction from me. Everything seemed to roll right off my back. My friends started saying that I was different: calmer, quieter, happier, and more peaceful. It wasn't an intellectual change—I didn't change the way I thought—it was almost a physical change, affecting my natural responses to everything. I felt a new sense of detachment. Getting in touch with an inner sense of calmness, peace, and tranquillity, for only a few minutes every day, brought some of that peacefulness into my conscious life the rest of the time.

Zen monks meditate—sit *zazen*—for hours, sometimes days at a time. They meditate indoors or out in nature, silently or chanting, alone or in groups, sometimes focused on a *koen*, a Zen riddle designed to achieve stillness of mind. They devote their lives to achieving enlightenment through Zen practice, including (but not limited to) meditation. While the rest of us have many other activities and pursuits taking up a lot of our time, we can get a lot out of just practicing meditation techniques. We can experience another, more open, attentive, and spiritual way of being, and carry this into all areas of our lives.

Over the years, I did not stick with my original meditation practices as faithfully as I might have. I moved on to follow other paths and learn many different techniques of meditation and creative visualization. But I still find myself returning to the simplest forms, the most basic efforts to still my mind, focus my concentration, and *be here now*. In all my explorations of Buddhism, Taoism, tai chi, the I Ching (fortune-telling oracle), and *Feng Shui* (awareness of the energy flow patterns formed by the placement of objects), I have learned the same basic lessons: awareness of and full participation in each present moment; the oneness of the energy flowing through me, my garden, and everything in the universe; everything I need to know is already inside me; everything is perfect, exactly as it is; the ebb and flow of energy in the universe is constantly creating balance and harmony.

One of the I Ching hexagrams is called The Well, and it describes the infinite well of truth and energy that exists throughout the universe. It describes a water well that continues to exist no matter what happens to the town or its people; it remains unchanged through war and hardship, abundance and poverty, for countless generations. Whatever happens in ourselves, our lives, or the world, there is a well that is endlessly full, always ready to enrich and refresh us. This is how I like to think of meditation: as going to the infinite, eternal well for a sip of that which is real, true, and unchanging, everywhere and forever. Only by allowing emptiness within us, can we be filled up anew.

Meditation puts us in touch with our true connection to the rest of the universe, our oneness with it. The garden is a perfect, natural setting in which to discover and practice this awareness. Sitting in my garden, on the grass, under the trees, I let go of all thoughts and desires and open up to the consciousness of the universe. Counting my breath gives me focus and concentration. Observing the thoughts that sneak back into my mind keeps me detached from them. I am one with all of nature around me and inside me, all that can be seen and heard and all that cannot be seen or heard. I am nothing, and I am everything. Since enlightenment exists in the universe, I am enlightened.

After meditating, I always feel more calm, peaceful, and aware. Everything seems wonderful, beautiful, and filled with life. I accept everything, and I love everything. Just sitting in my garden takes me out of myself and brings me back to my true, essential self. Irritations, worries, and problems seem unimportant. A sense of balance and well-being pervades. Nothing in the world changes, but I see and approach everything differently.

But meditation is not the only way to sit Zen in the garden. You can just sit, looking, listening, opening up to whatever is there in the present moment. You can sit in a chair or on the ground, with your eyes open or closed. You can sit in your garden when you're tired or alert, happy or sad, ready to meditate or unable to focus. All you have to do is *just sit*, all you have to be is open. Whenever you go to the universe with an empty bowl, it is always generously filled.

CREATURES GREAT AND SMALL

Few men have souls so dead that they will not even bother to look up when they hear the barking of wild Geese.

—Roger Tory Peterson

Butterfly, flower, and my eyes are one.

—Mobi Ho

Summer sky
clear after rain
ants on parade.

—Shiki

Greenfly, it's difficult to see
Why God, who made the rose, made thee.

—A. P. Herbert

On every stem, on every leaf and at the root of everything that grew, was a professional specialist in

the shape of grub, caterpillar, aphis, or other expert,
whose business it was to devour that particular part.
—Oliver Wendell Holmes

The garden is a world teeming with life. While the cicadas hum and birds sing overhead, the ground is a busy city filled with creatures rushing here and there, going about their daily tasks. Squirrels, chipmunks, moles, rabbits, cats, and raccoons roam the neighborhood; butterflies, bees, ants, mosquitos, aphids, dragonflies, worms, slugs, caterpillars, grubs, and ladybugs fly and crawl everywhere. I have mixed feelings about sharing my garden with them. On one hand, it is perfectly correct and natural for them to be here; on the other, they're eating my leaves and vegetables!

I saw a brazen squirrel digging up my baby carrots yesterday. He must be the one who's been leaving holes in the soil everywhere I look. Or maybe that's the little chipmunk who lives under my deck. Counting my blessings, I would have to admit that I haven't had any trouble with rabbits or raccoons this year, as I have in the past. My Siberian husky got into a fight with a vicious raccoon who was trying to raid my vegetable garden one year. She had to have shots and we had to build a new fence. Raccoons are cute in pictures, but you don't want them around in real life.

Generally, I don't mind sharing my garden with the little animals, and I always grow a little extra with this in mind. But this year I have lost an unusual amount of vegetables due to them and their insect relatives. I'm not happy about giving up my peppers and zucchinis altogether and a fair amount of my cucumbers and carrots to greedy, virus-carrying creatures. Sometimes animals and insects are actually good for the garden; sometimes they're harmless to it; and sometimes they're just pests.

Early in the season, when I had a lot of work to do getting the garden started, I was bothered by lots of flying insects. I bought a couple of large citronella candles and burned them beside me as I worked. This had a pretty good effect, and I was glad not to use any chemical sprays or anything like that. In setting up my garden, I tried to use all kinds of natural means to keep the insects under control: marigolds, garlic and onions, herbs, and petunias. I considered buying one of those new mosquito-repelling plants, but in Minnesota, with all our lakes, I would have to have filled the backyard with them.

As I filled my raised beds with compost, peat moss, and soil, I discovered that some of the bagged topsoil I bought was filled with ants! Something I did—the petunias, marigolds, garlic, or onions—must have worked on them, because they disappeared quickly. Ladybugs helped with the aphids, and pepper spray kept my tomatoes free of most of the natural pests they attract.

Our relationships with the creatures in our garden are more problematic than our relationships with the plant life there. While our plants may disappoint us (usually because of something *we've* done wrong), the animals and insects are only doing what is natural for them to do—fulfilling their essential natures—when they steal our food and spoil our gardens. So what do we do? Kill them? Screw up the balance of nature by destroying a natural part of it?

I don't like killing anything. Insects and small garden animals may have a limited capacity for consciousness, but they are alive, a natural part of the ecosystem. While all of our landscaping and gardening is not quite the most natural state for our property to be in, our influence on and participation in the nature all around us should be helpful, not harmful. We can cultivate the earth without screwing it up. When we recognize our place in the ecosystem, our interconnectedness with everything else in it, we can grow and harvest all we need to without harming the animal and insect life.

Our relationships with animals in natural settings are filled with all kinds of old information we have stored away in our minds: old personal experiences and tales we have been told. I recoil at the buzz of a bee because of a bad sting I experienced as a small child. Squirrels remind me of stories I heard about vicious, rabid ones biting people's hands in urban parks—a habit they developed because people tried to feed them peanuts and popcorn out of their hands. Insects creep us out, and we think nothing of killing them.

A friend recently returned from a vacation where people must keep an ever-watchful eye out for poisonous snakes and insects. The people he was staying with had to kill a three-inch scorpion that had somehow gotten into their baby's room. That story made my struggle with garden creatures pale in comparison. Ground squirrels may eat my carrots and aphids may ruin my tomatoes and peppers, but they won't kill me or my family. We need to keep things in perspective when it comes to dealing with animals and insects in the garden. We need to think about the place and purpose of every living thing in nature before we do anything to it.

Zen monks contemplate a butterfly or ant and discover they are one with it. Geese fly overhead, and we marvel at their instinctive

migration, telling us of the changing seasons. Chipmunks and squirrels run back and forth, filling their secret nests with food for the
coming months. Bees buzz around, pollinating as they go. It is all
interconnected, one world full of little animals, including us. We are
more than relatives to the creatures who share our earth; we are them
and they are us. There is only one energy flowing through us all.

We must protect ourselves from raccoons and scorpions, pre-
venting confrontations with them as much as we can. But we can also
learn to live harmoniously with most, if not all, of the creatures in
our gardens. They are truly no more annoying to us than we are to
one another or ourselves. They are no more deserving of mass gen-
ocide for sharing our harvest than we are for invading their natural
habitat. We can all live together peacefully when we know who we
both are in the larger scheme of things. The creatures, great and small,
that share our gardens are one with the plants there and with us. We
all need each other.

The next time you see a bird or chipmunk on your lawn, look at
it with new eyes. See its life force, the energy that connects it to you.
Listen to its story and its wisdom. Offer your aphids nasturtiums to
feed on as an alternative to your tomatoes. Use chalk to keep your
ants where they won't harm your plants—they won't cross a chalk
line. Interact with the creatures in your garden, instead of trying to
control or dominate them. Develop a relationship of peace and harmony with them. Give them what they need, and they will leave
enough for you. When they are healthy and happy, so is your garden.
So are you. And so are we all.

RECYCLING

Garbage becomes rose
Rose becomes compost—
Everything is in transformation.
Even permanence is impermanent.

—Thich Nhat Hanh

Life lives on life.
We all eat and are eaten.
When we forget this, we cry;
when we remember it,
we can nourish one another.

—Jack Kornfield

Nature is cyclical. Everything in the living world passes through endless stages of birth, life, death, and rebirth. Everything can be and is used by other things; life supports life. All the stems, leaves, and flowers that grow in my garden end up dead, dried, decomposed, and back in the soil to enrich the next crop. Weeds, damaged fruits and vegetables, and kitchen scraps are ground up, composted, and returned to the earth. Even diseased plants can often be composted and turned into fertilizer for healthy soil.

It's amazing to me that when I was growing up, no one ever used the word *recycle*. Aluminum soda and beer cans weren't used much, but when they were, we simply threw them out with the rest of the trash: paper, food waste, plastic, batteries, whatever. Soda (but not wine or beer) bottles were returnable for refunds, and some people saved their used aluminum foil and cans to get a few cents from the trash man, but mostly, we just put out the garbage and forgot about it. We lived with the illusion that natural resources were unlimited and garbage could simply be dumped somewhere and forgotten.

Now that we are more aware of the cycles of nature, the need for conservation and replenishment of natural resources, our relationship with the earth has changed. We are closer to recognizing and fulfilling our true, essential nature, our correct place in the living planet and universe. We are able to be less harmful and more helpful within this role. But it does require a little more consciousness and effort.

In the garden, we can easily recycle organic matter by composting. The more we chop up or grind the stems, leaves, fruits, and vegetables before we compost them, the faster they will break down. A composter is really quite an amazing thing; it magically transforms garbage into rich, black fertilizer. This resulting material can be spread on the garden as mulch before the winter sets in, or in the spring, beneath layers of peat moss and topsoil. The minerals and nutrients in all those plants are put back into the soil instead of discarded. They become part of the next bed of flowers or patch of vegetables. When you eat this year's tomatoes, you may be ingesting some of the iron from last year's nettles.

Being a harmless and helpful part of the cycles of nature changes many of our habits and chores. It takes a little more time to sort trash and prepare compost, and it's often less pleasant to have to deal with garbage than to just throw it away. As hard as it is for many of us to retrain ourselves to stop and smell the flowers—to be fully present in every beautiful moment—it's even harder for us to be attentive and mindful about sorting garbage, stirring compost, or cleaning up dog droppings.

However, such chores can be perfect opportunities for Zen practice. We are never more inclined to do things quickly and carelessly than when we find the task at hand somehow unpleasant. Dirty and smelly chores don't seem like something we'd want to do slowly or attentively, but when we do them that way, peacefully, acceptingly, fully conscious of the part of nature's cycles in which we are participating, we change our minds about what they are and our relationships with them. I don't actually like cleaning up my dog's area of the backyard, but I don't mind it as much as I used to. I do it thinking about the interconnectedness of all life, including me, my dog, and all the earth and plant life around me. I try to do it the way I would perform a tea ceremony or tend my garden.

When my family became vegetarian, one of the first effects we noticed was that our garbage didn't smell as bad. Without any animal products, our trash consisted almost entirely of paper and vegetable food scraps. We no longer had a garbage disposal, and discovered how much organic matter we had been washing down the drain.

That's when we started composting not just garden matter, but kitchen waste as well.

You can't compost animal products, nuts, dairy products, or eggshells, or anything with mayonnaise, salad dressing, butter, oil, or a sauce (such as baked beans). We don't compost pasta, rice dishes, or packaged soups. Eating foods closer to their natural state is better for our bodies as well as our compost. We've found that grinding up vegetable scraps in a blender before adding them to the composter makes it break down much faster. Using a weed whacker inside a trash can filled with grass clippings and other garden waste to chop it up, and adding soil and stirring the compost frequently, also aids quick decomposition.

By composting, recycling cans, bottles, and plastic containers, and burning most of our paper trash, we have reduced our garbage considerably. Stale bread is fed to the birds, geese, and ducks that live in our area, and batteries are brought to the local recycling pick-up station for proper, safe disposal. Through mindful participation in nature's cycles, we have completely changed our family's impact on the earth. By performing these chores as Zen practice, we have discovered our true relationship to and place within the ongoing cycles of nature all around us.

Another method of recycling your kitchen scraps is feeding them to a box of worms kept specifically for this purpose. I haven't tried this myself, but I'm told it works wonderfully well. Human creativity and inventiveness is one of our most important contributions to the planet. We are capable of recognizing and solving problems, and of making changes based on new information, new attitudes, and new technology. As we learn more and more about the needs and care of the earth, we can become a more consciously positive part of it.

When we approach even the most menial chores with the Zen attitude of openness, attentiveness, peacefulness, and care, they are transformed. When we recognize our responsibilities within the complex systems of nature, we learn its supremely simple truth: that we are one with the animal and plant life, the stone, sand, and soil, the air and water of the earth; that when we join in nature's rhythms and cycles instead of fighting or ignoring them, we improve life for all of us.

FLOWERS

The earth laughs in flowers.
—Ralph Waldo Emerson

Bread feeds the body indeed, but flowers feed also the soul.
—The Koran

O world, as God has made it! All is beauty.
—Robert Browning

I perhaps owe having become a painter to flowers.
—Claude Monet

A thing of beauty is a joy forever.
—John Keats

These roses under my window make no reference to former roses or to better ones; they are for what they are; they exist with God to-day. There is no time to them. There is simply the rose; it is perfect in every moment of its existence.

—Ralph Waldo Emerson

Flowers are restful to look at. They have neither emotions nor conflicts.

—Sigmund Freud

Blossoms perform many functions in nature. They precede fruits and vegetables on vines and stalks; they provide medicinal herbs; they invite butterflies and hummingbirds into our gardens; many of their petals and seeds are edible; and they grace our gardens, homes, and world with beauty, both visual and fragrant. While many other plants provide us with nourishment and medicine, what would the world be like without the beauty of flowers?

The beauty of flowers touches us on a deep, natural level. It speaks to our hearts and souls, our essential natures. It pleases our minds and emotions with harmony, balance, unity, and peace. It calls to our spirits, and we respond with natural joy. While our culture seems obsessed with style and fashion, it also seems to grossly underestimate the importance of real beauty. We absorb, internalize, and are an inseparable part of our surroundings: we become one with ugliness or beauty, wherever we are.

The beauty of nature is the most perfectly balanced and pleasing to us all, as well as the most accessible and inexpensive. We can visit parks, conservatories, arboretums, greenhouses, and garden centers; we can buy a tiny pack of seeds for about a dollar and grow a whole bed of fabulous flowers. We can bring nature's beauty into our buildings, on windowsills or in window boxes. We can urge beauty out of the smallest bit of earth available to us. If we're fortunate enough to have more space and soil, we can fill our world with an abundance of beautiful color and fragrance.

Over the years, I have grown lilies, marigolds, impatiens, geraniums, lilacs, hydrangeas, coneflowers, gladioli, bleeding hearts, snapdragons, azaleas, rhododendrons, petunias, chrysanthemums, bachelor's buttons, irises, phlox, daisies, pansies, alyssum, nasturtiums, sweet peas, asters, zinnias, begonias, peonies, and sunflowers. I have been surrounded by many different varieties of hosta and helped clematis, morning glories, sweet peas, and roses climb up trellises, trees, and lampposts. I have been lucky enough to host many other varieties of flowers I don't even know or remember the names of, and to visit a countless number of other gardens filled with beautiful blossoms of every description. They have all given me the wonderful gift of beauty.

I confess that, because of my old fear of bees, I have always thought of flowers as bee magnets, and that probably has something to do with my preference for herb and vegetable gardening. But nothing stuns my senses into reverential awe like a bed of bright, healthy, happy flowers. Their beauty is inescapable and universal. Growing them brings incomparable rewards.

I have always had better luck growing annuals than perennials. Perhaps it is partly due to the very cold winters here, destroying all but the hardiest varieties. It always seems more cost-effective to buy perennials, even though they're much more expensive than annuals.

But if they last for years to come, propagating themselves into even more plants, it seems logical to buy them instead of less-expensive annuals that only live for one season. Nonetheless, my annuals always look fabulous, while my perennials tend to have good years and bad years, great foliage and not much in the way of flowers, or great flowers that only last a short time and then leave behind feeble-looking foliage.

Growing perennials is a long-term project: you have to be pretty well rooted where you are, and able to plan your garden ahead for several years. Some perennials only bloom every other year; some need to be split and transplanted every three or four years; and some need a lot of fertilizing and fussing over. A perennial garden develops over the years, revealing more and more of the gardener's vision and soul. It illustrates the interconnectedness of all life, not only in space, but in time—past, present, and future.

Annuals are a different story. Their lives are brief; they have a one-shot chance at expressing all the beauty and life they possibly can. And, in my experience, they make the most of it. With a minimum of information, you can give your annuals everything they need to flourish. Impatiens thrive in the shade, and when wilted by too much heat or sun, pop right back up with some watering. Marigolds like sunshine and need to have their deadheads popped off almost every day in the height of the season. Asters, zinnias, gladioli, and daisies are wonderful for cutting and bringing indoors to brighten up any room or table setting for days, but daylilies last exactly one day off the stalk, whether or not they're in water.

Coleus is not exactly a flower, but it is so pretty and colorful that it is grown for its beauty along with flowering plants. Its red, green, and creamy white leaves come in all variations and shapes, flat and curly. It's one of my favorite annuals because it's so easy to grow and fits in nicely with so many other plants. The variety that grows deep red leaves with green edges accents white flower beds beautifully. Other varieties include variegated leaves with white and green, red and green, and red, white, and green.

Some people like to wait for their perennials to come back and then fill in any bare spaces between them with annuals, creating a different-looking garden every year. Other people keep their perennial and annual beds completely separate. Since some flowers bloom early in the season and others later, it's possible to have a continuously changing, blossoming flower garden all season by planting early and late varieties together. From the first crocus, daffodils, and tulips, through the rhododendrons, viola, petunias, geraniums, lilies, and marigolds, to the autumn chrysanthemums, the beauty of your flower garden never wanes. On the other hand, a bed full of just one variety and color of flower can be dramatically beautiful.

Flowers are nature's gift to us and nature's joy for itself. Since we and nature are one in the same, loving flowers and appreciating their beauty is natural for us. It is the essential nature of the flower to be beautiful; it is part of the essential nature of humans to love beauty. When we let nature surround us with this beauty, it can bring us peace and joy. It can make our interactions with the earth happier and more harmonious. The natural life energy that flows through us also flows through flowers and their beauty. When we are living Zen, they are us and we are them, one beautiful earthly garden.

HERBS

I wonder: can anyone rationally suggest there is no order to the universe when there are such small potent miracles as herbs abroad?

—Dorothy Gilman

For you there's rosemary and rue; these keep Seeming and savor all winter long.

—William Shakespeare

Gardening with herbs, which is becoming increasingly popular, is indulged in by those who like subtlety in their plants in preference to brilliance.

—Helen Morgenthau Fox

I plant rosemary all over the garden, so pleasant is it to know that at every few steps one may draw the kindly branchlets through one's hand, and have the enjoyment of their incomparable incense.

—Gertrude Jekyll

Herbs have been important throughout human history. Besides adding flavor to foods, they have been used for medicinal, decorative, cosmetic, and magical purposes. People have enjoyed their wonderful scents in both fresh and dried form, and soothing teas have been popular for hundreds of years. Herbs have a long history of helping people in many ways: homeopathy (or natural medicine practiced by a qualified medical herbalist), first aid or home remedies, and natural cosmetics for hair and skin.

It's difficult to say exactly which of our garden treasures should be called herbs. Generally, we think of herbs as those plants that we can use for seasoning our food (such as sage, basil, and thyme), making teas (chamomile and peppermint), and taking as dietary supplements (echinacea, ginseng, and garlic). But all kinds of plants give us herbal home remedies and spice up our foods: plants that we usually think of as flowers, roots, berries, weeds, and vegetables. Cayenne peppers, alliums (onions, leeks, garlic, and chives), horseradish, roses (petals and hips), sunflowers (seeds and flowers), geraniums, stinging nettles, dandelions, and strawberries could all be called herbs.

Herbs also have cosmetic uses in such preparations as skin toners, lotions, and cleansers; facial masks; shampoos and hair conditioners; hand creams; foot fresheners and deodorizers; toothpastes and mouthwashes; and soothing, scented baths. Roses, lavender, rosemary, mints, parsley, yarrow, sage, calendula, comfrey, chamomile, and nettles can be grown for these purposes. Some herbs are grown strictly for their scent or cosmetic properties, and are not safe to eat or use in cooking or teas. Marigolds, soapwort, poppies (except the seeds), and aloe vera are some examples of these herbs.

Growing herbs is one of the most pleasurable experiences a gardener can have. The sweet, spicy scent that rises up when I spray them with water is reason enough for me to devote a good portion of my garden to these plants. Aromatherapy is one of those ancient-wisdom practices now getting a lot of attention and interest; scientific studies are proving its effectiveness in worker productivity, weight loss, treatment of pain and depression, and many other areas.

But I also use herbs for many other purposes: chamomile and peppermint teas; a few sprigs of rosemary in my bathwater; basil, oregano, garlic, onions, and Italian parsley in all my pasta dishes; dill leaves in sour cream for veggie dip and cream cheese for cracker spread; and chives in sour cream on baked potatoes. I collect marigold, rose, geranium, lavender, rosemary, primrose, mint, thyme, basil, and sage to dry for a variety of potpourris and sachets.

Preserving herbs for cooking is easy. I have used two different methods, both successfully. One method is to pick and wash the leaves (of basil, sage, rosemary, or thyme), dry them gently with a towel or paper towel, and lay them out on newspaper to dry. You can also use mesh screen of some sort, allowing air circulation all around the leaves (those contraptions for laying out clothes to dry are good for this). Or you can spread them out on newspaper on a cookie sheet and keep them in an oven when you're not using it (just make sure it's off!). This works for either electric or gas ovens, but the pilot light of a gas ovens will speed up the drying process (my grandmother has always used this method for drying peppers). Herbs for potpourris can be dried in the same manner.

The other method of preserving herbs for cooking is freezing. Pick the leaves, wash and dry them thoroughly, and place them in freezer bags or layered between paper towels in plastic containers. Make small batches, so you can use them immediately when you take them out of the freezer. They also chop much more easily when they're still frozen. I prefer this method for parsley and chives, while I usually dry basil, rosemary, bay (laurel), and thyme. If you are going to use them up quickly, you can keep fresh herbs in the refrigerator in cheesecloth bags or plastic bags with holes in them. They'll stay fresh longer if you wait to wash them until you're ready to use them.

Herbs can be found at many grocery stores and all health food stores, but I am fortunate enough to live in a city that actually has an herb store. They sell herb capsules and herbal incense and oils, as well as fresh herbs mixed by a trained herbalist, who is always available to answer questions and give advice. I have learned a great deal about the herbs I grow on my visits to this shop, particularly about their medicinal properties: echinacea helps build up our immune system; garlic is good for colds, coughs, and laryngitis; ginger and ginseng help nausea; cayenne is good for circulatory and digestive problems; chamomile tea helps everything from tension to insomnia to stomachaches. Since some herbs can be very dangerous when ingested, it's important to consult knowledgeable sources before using them in cooking or as dietary supplements.

Today, herbs also come to us with centuries of folklore behind them. Legends and stories, and magical properties and spells are attached to many of the herbs we still grow. Protection from harm, knowledge of the future, and attracting love, money, and good luck have all been attributed to herbs. Ancient wisdom associates herbs with rituals that cleanse the human mind and heart and give them new focus. Herbs have been used in everything from the ancient Zen tea ceremony to modern Christian rituals. Humans have always known the power of herbs to affect our minds, hearts, spirits, and lives.

Every year I plan to grow more herbs the next year. But somehow, in the spring madness of garden centers and seed catalogues, herbs tend to get lost in the shuffle of all those flower and vegetable plants. I always grow certain herbs that I use a lot in cooking: mints, basil, garlic, onions, chives, sage, rosemary, oregano, and parsley. Every year I try a few others, such as thyme, bay, dill, chamomile, and lavender. I usually grow a little catnip for my cats. I grow my potpourri flowers in with my other perennials and annuals (except for marigolds, which I grow throughout the garden).

Next year, I want a large and complete traditional herb garden. Maybe I'll give up growing some vegetables and use one of my raised beds for nothing else. I'll grow more varieties than I ever have before. I'll tend them with greater concentration, attentiveness, and care than anything I have ever grown. I will use them for everything for which they can possibly be used. I'll make lots of herbal teas, sachets, and potpourris. I'll dry and freeze tons of herbs for cooking. I'll put rosemary and lavender in my pillows and dresser drawers. I'll make catnip sachets for my cats.

My daughter wants to bring potted rosemary and basil plants with her when she goes back to living in her college dorm when summer is over. She loves the scents they bring into a room, the bit of earthiness, the closeness to nature. Whether we use them for cooking, health, or cosmetic purposes, herbs bring us closer to our true, natural selves. They speak to us on a deep, primal level. They remind us of our oneness with the earth from which they spring. They can be used for so many things and affect us in so many ways and areas of our lives that we feel the energy of the earth running through us, our gardens, and our lives all day long. Herbs are the physical thread that connects every part of ourselves and our lives to the earth and the universe. And tending them is one of the greatest joys in the garden.

ABUNDANT HARVEST

*K**nowing so little brought surprise after surprise: the way broccoli grows, designed by some celestial order to send out great leaves, and grow until it's the size of a basketball; the dark green curling leaves of spinach, ruffled like curtains; the fantastic horn-shaped flowers of the zucchini, with its two different kinds of leaves; the silky tassels of corn; the fragrance of English lavender and basil and sage. And for all this I had planted only one seed, and then another and another.*

—Dorothy Gilman

Fruit falls from the tree when it is ripe.

—Jack Kornfield

In nature there are neither rewards nor punishments—there are consequences.

—Robert G. Ingersoll

As ye sow, so shall ye reap.

—The Holy Bible

Late in the season, the garden changes. It begins to show its age, its weariness, and its resignation to the coming autumn. Colors fade, vines appear limp and bedraggled, burdened by the weight of their fruits and vegetables. When the garden no longer looks its best, comes harvest time.

We harvest lettuces, beans, and other vegetables earlier in the summer; succession planting in some cases, harvesting several times from the same plants in others. But as the summer begins to wane, those long-awaited tomatoes ripen—zillions of them all at once—and must be picked. Carrots, leeks, squash, and eggplant are also late bloomers where I live. August and September are busy months for the kitchen gardener. With all this abundance coming forth at once, we have to eat, give away, or put up our harvest in a hurry.

Eating is easy. Nothing in any grocery store tastes quite like veggies that come straight from the earth in our gardens. Our fresh produce is delicious in stir-fries and salads, steamed or raw. Sweet corn makes its annual appearance for a few weeks, and cucumbers (I always grow the burpless variety) ripen by the bushel for many wonderful salads and sandwiches. Green beans, carrots, onions, broccoli, Brussels sprouts, and cabbages keep us well-fed for weeks. Giving some away is part of the joy of gardening, and for some people, its main purpose. We can each only eat so much of nature's bounty, but the gardening process is so enjoyable that we end up growing enough for an army.

Besides enjoying my own harvest, I like to go to the farmers' markets at this time of year to see what other people have managed to coax forth from the earth. I buy the things I haven't grown myself, thereby negating the "we'll save on grocery money by growing our own vegetables" line I deliver every spring. My neighbors ply me with home-grown strawberries and peppers (having sympathetically heard of my disastrous attempt to grow them this year), hoping to be reciprocated with gifts of my tomatoes and cucumbers. The state fair brings thousands of people in search of the best specimens of plants and vegetables around. We all get into the spirit of harvest time.

I have lived through many harvests, each of them a little different. One year, corn is expensive because the crop was all but ruined by excessive rainfall, and the next year, it's abundant and cheap. Sometimes I have grown bushels of zucchini, ranging from six to sixteen inches in length. I have, in response, collected several great recipes for zucchini bread. I have pickled beets in sweet syrup and filled my freezer with blanched green beans. I have persuaded my daughter (when she was little) to eat a crop of Brussels sprouts simply by calling them "baby cabbages" instead. I have mixed salad greens until I couldn't stand them any more and canned tomatoes until the wallpaper in my kitchen began peeling from the steam.

This year, I've grown fewer different varieties of vegetables than I have before. There will be no need for zucchini bread recipes (unless I find a gorgeous supply at the farmers' market), and we've already eaten up the green beans and cucumbers. I do have several beautiful deep-purple eggplants still growing that I think will be my special memorable crop from this season. Every season has one of those for me, and it's always different. While a bad tomato year is unheard of in my house, I have suffered poor showings of just about everything else in my garden at one time or another. But every year something (besides my tomatoes) always astonishes me with its beautiful abundance.

For a few weeks we eat lots of fresh veggies, give them away, and preserve them in a variety of fashions. The season is winding down, the garden is clearing out. Bare ground is replacing that jungle of vegetable plants that has graced my backyard for months now. Another cycle is completing, a new one will begin. But before we need to think about covering our perennials with mulch to protect them from cold temperatures, there is one more joyful moment left on the harvest clock.

Apples! I have always loved autumn: trees turning from green to yellow to a blaze of red and orange; cooler temperatures and crisp fresh air; dry leaves crunching underfoot. But the best part of the fall season is apples: apple fritters, apple pies, applesauce, apple butter, and apple cider and donuts. I can recall their scent and flavor just thinking about them. Autumn is apple season, and where I have lived, in the Midwest, apples are everywhere.

Only once have I had an apple tree of my own. It bore an abundance of fruit, the kind especially good for cooking: slightly tart and rather soft in texture. I stood on a ladder, picking the apples on the lower branches that hadn't fallen on their own. I baked pies and cooked applesauce and apple butter on the stove. The house smelled heavenly for days. Another place I lived had a town nearby with orchards and annual apple festivals. I haunted the quaint shops there for fresh cider and chutney. Where I live now, my apples all come from farmers' markets and grocery stores. But they still mark the beginning of autumn and make me feel great.

Harvest time is the time for reaping what we have sown over the past months, for getting back the loving energy we have given our gardens. Our successes and failures culminate in their natural results. But there is no blame in nature's way; everything turned out perfectly in accordance with what I did and didn't do, along with all the natural factors affecting this year's garden. Nature neither rewards nor punishes us, it simply acts in perfect harmony. What we give our gardens comes back to us multiplied. Kindness, compassion, respect, peacefulness and mindful attention create more wonderful results than all the horticultural expertise in the world. Our gardens are blameless and so are we; we have simply interacted for a season and harvested the results. We don't have to be thankful for nature just doing what it does naturally, for following the laws of earthly nature and of karma (what goes around, comes around; you reap what you sow). But somehow, at harvest time, we find that we are indeed, very thankful.

LITTLE BUDDHAS

We don't know who our teachers are until we have been taught.

—James P. Carse

All things are full of signs, and it is a wise man who can learn about one thing from another.

—Plotinus

Come forth into the light of things,
Let Nature be your teacher.

—William Wordsworth

You will find something more in woods than in books. Trees and stones will teach you that which you can never learn from masters.

—St. Bernard

Go forth under the open sky and listen to Nature's teachings.

—William Cullen Bryant

I went to the woods because I wished to live
deliberately, to front only the essential facts of life,
and see if I could not learn what it had to teach.
                              —Henry David Thoreau

Gardening is a multifaceted experience. We use our imaginations, our uniquely human ability to plan, design, and decide; we work to make our plans reality, giving something of ourselves, our time, energy, and helpfulness to the earth; we receive health, food, beauty, and peacefulness in return; we learn, grow, and change as we allow the earth to teach us important lessons. A relentless teacher, nature gives us an endless supply of experiences designed to help us in the garden and everywhere else. Every success and failure; every seed, sprout, and flower; every tomato, pepper, and cucumber; every chipmunk, squirrel, ant, aphid, bird, and butterfly; all the compost, peat moss, and topsoil—they are all "Little Buddhas" or teachers for us.

Through our Zen gardening experiences, we learn lessons in patience, acceptance, openness, and flexibility; we develop skills in listening, seeing, and communicating; we become more aware of reality and our place in it. In the garden, we learn the necessity of peaceful activity and interaction, of nonresistance and following the natural flow of energy. We find evidence of our interconnectedness with the earth and all other beings. We begin to accept the cycles and seasons of life, the ever-changing nature of all nature. We let go of our expectations and desires and discover pleasant surprises. We see proof of life's most basic, simple, and important truths.

One of these basic truths is called *karma*. In our Western culture, we know this as the rule, *what goes around, comes around*. But this view implies a judgment not present in the Zen concept of karma. Zen gardening teaches us that the law of karma is not one of crimes and punishments, but rather of simple causes and effects, actions and their natural results. We are always creating the future in each present moment; this is the correct and natural way of all life, the world, and the universe.

Another simple truth we can learn through our Zen gardening experiences is called *wu-wei*, or nonaction. In Zen, we learn to not act, but to be still and wait, listening for the correct action or answer to reveal itself to us. When we are open to sensing the natural flow of the energy running all around and through us, we can find the correct path by following that energy rather than trying to control or lead it. Instead of trying to force our own beliefs and desires onto nature, we yield to it, allowing it to unfold, and discovering our own correct part in it.

Before anything new can come to you, you have to make an empty space for it. In practicing wu-wei, we cease all action, creating an empty space that can be filled by the correct, natural action. In practicing beginner's mind, we create space in our minds and hearts for new ideas, feelings, and attitudes to enter. In the expert's mind there are only rigid beliefs and ideas, no empty space or room for any new information. Beginner's mind is open, accepting, and ready for new information to enter into it.

The basic truth of interconnectedness of all life teaches us of the ripple effects of everything in the universe, affecting everything else. We learn to think about our interdependence with all other life forms all over the world. In the garden, we learn to be responsible for the effects of our actions on everything else, and begin to see how everything else affects us. We discover our place in the larger ecosystems, the food chain, the universal energy flow. We discover our oneness with the one energy that flows throughout the earth and universe.

Zen gardening teaches us mindfulness, the importance of awareness, and attentive actions. We learn to be fully focused, here and now, on whatever we are doing. We become one with all the natural materials in the garden, and with the flow of energy in the work in which we are participating. We lose our ego-selves in concentrated effort that comes from our true, essential selves.

The true, essential nature of everything is revealed to us in Zen gardening. We learn to recognize and respect the reality of each part of our garden: plants, animals, soil, trees, air, water, and sunlight. If it is the essential nature of a plant to grow best in the shade, it is disrespectful to plant it in full sun; if a squirrel's essential nature is to find its food on the ground, we can hardly be surprised or unhappy when it shares our garden vegetables. Our own true essential nature is also revealed to us in relation to the rest of nature, and we grow to know and respect it as well.

In Zen gardening, we learn humility, simplicity, compassion, detachment, and nonresistance. We learn to accept the balance, the constant ebb and flow—or yin and yang—of life. We get more and more peaceful, relaxed, and serene. We come to believe that everything is perfect, just as it is. We find change and surprise less threatening, expectations and desires more foolish and simply unnecessary. Everything will unfold exactly as it should: blossoming and dying, wilting and dying, living and dying. The Zen gardener learns to accept all.

The word *buddha* literally means *enlightened one*. We observe, follow, and learn from the enlightened ones among us. We become quiet and listen to them with open minds and hearts. We empty ourselves out and take in what they can teach us. From a seedling, we may learn patience; from a squirrel, we may learn industry; from a summer day, we may learn peace and joy; from a flower, we may learn beauty; from a nesting bird, we may learn focus and concentration. A tornado may teach us acceptance and flexibility; a fallen tree limb may teach us about life cycles and letting go of the past gracefully.

Buddhas come in all forms, shapes, and sizes. They don't teach in the way we're used to being taught, by preaching, instructing, telling, and testing. They simply are themselves, true to their essential natures, and by observing them with openness, with beginner's mind, we learn. And in learning, the whole rest of the world learns along with us, because we are one world, one energy, one life force, one universe. We are all Little Buddhas.

SAME TIME, NEXT YEAR

Even the seasons form a great circle in their changing, and always come back again to where they were.

—Black Elk

*We have had our summer evenings,
now for October eves!*

—Humbert Wolfe

*O Wind,
If Winter comes, can spring be far behind?*
—Percy Bysshe Shelley

*The grim frost is at hand, when the apples will fall
thick, almost thunderous, on the hardened earth.*
—D. H. Lawrence

As this year in my garden winds down, as I clean up the vegetable plants and harvest the herbs, I think about what I have learned from my garden this year. Lessons in patience, acceptance, calmness, and attentiveness come to mind. Experiences of communion with nature and losing myself in the oneness of all living energy flood my memory. Scents and colors fill my mind, remembering this season in my garden. I have received so much more than I gave.

After another season of gardening, I now have more faith and optimism in the future. I have learned both practical lessons from the earth and lessons about my own mental, emotional, and spiritual presence in the garden. Unlike so many other lessons in life, which make us wonder why we had to go through so much to learn something we'll probably never get to use in this lifetime, spiritual lessons are always valuable, and practical garden lessons can always be used next year.

A garden is years in the making, constantly evolving, even if its stewardship changes. We move so often now, that we may garden many different places in a lifetime. But each garden remains, accepting changes every year: a new plant here, a different arrangement there. The garden grows and diminishes over time, a living organism, with as full a life as its caretakers. It hosts various plants, animals, and insects; it adapts to drought and flood, care and neglect, and the whims of human intervention. The garden lives its life, with or without us.

In a season, we can learn to be better at participating in the life of our garden. We can find our place in the natural cycles and patterns of the living earth and allow nature's energy to run freely through us and use us to be helpful and not harmful to the garden. We can learn to let go of our human ego's fears and doubts, freeing us to develop our own natural green thumb. And we can carry all of the lessons our garden shares with us into every other area of life, because it is all a single, connected, continuous energy chain.

Geese fly overhead, barking joyfully, as I plant bulbs for next spring's garden. Leaves have already begun falling from the giant trees all around. The garden looks weary and ready to rest for a while. My thoughts are filled with ideas, visions, and plans for next year. It's not that I feel dissatisfied with this year's garden; it has been perfect in every root and stem, every delicious tomato and fragrant herb, every smashing success and every mistake. But now it is nearly over, and the time has come to let it go. Now is the time for next year's garden to begin forming in my imagination.

Next year, I will grow more flowers; more of all the ones I grew this year, plus lots of new varieties. I will grow masses of impatiens in my shady spots, and mix in some new hosta, with more white leaves and blossoms. I'll add foxglove, lupins, white daisies, and purple coneflowers. I'll try hollyhocks and primrose. I want to have more trellises and arbors next year, bringing my garden up from the ground and above my head. Sweet peas, morning glories, roses, and clematis will climb trellises, arbors, fences, lampposts, and trees. In the sunniest spots, I'll grow lots of brightly colored annuals. This fall, I'll plant some lily and iris bulbs in with those I already have, to add even more foliage and color.

In my vegetable patch, I will trellis up the cucumbers and runner beans and tie up my tomato plants to eight-foot stakes earlier in the season. I'll try zucchini again and rotate the placement of my vegetable plants. I'll grow more varieties of salad greens and peppers (but not next to my tomatoes). I'll use marigolds, petunias, nasturtiums, and ladybugs to help keep my vegetables free of bugs and diseases. I probably won't try leeks again—their maturation time is much too long for this area—but I'll grow lots of onions and garlic, and definitely more eggplant. Maybe I'll grow broccoli and Brussels sprouts, cabbage and cauliflower—things I haven't grown in years. Or maybe I'll grow a lot fewer veggies and just more flowers.

Having learned so much about herbs this year, I will grow much more of them in next year's garden. I will have thick plots of lavender, mint, basil, and sage. I will have several rosemary bushes, because it is now my favorite herb in the garden. I will fill my raised beds with sand, compost, peat moss, and fresh soil. I'm thinking of building a little raised bed in the center of my raised beds, or maybe eliminating one or both of them, making more of my garden around the edges of my backyard. I might plant a red maple tree.

Just thinking about next year's garden makes me feel good. I walk through my backyard, imagining this and that, picturing in my mind an infinite array of possibilities. Every year is a new chance to start over, to begin at the beginning, planning, planting, building, and creating our gardens. Each year nature wipes the slate clean and lets us play all over again. Each year our garden can be completely different.

The Zen of gardening is simple: just do it. Just garden. Don't worry about being good enough or doing it right. Just do it with an open mind and heart, with a sense of joy and peacefulness, with attention and mindfulness. Instead of working on your garden, let your garden work on you. Live through a whole season with your garden, from the first seed catalog to the last October pumpkin. Nothing about it will be perfect, and yet everything about it will be.

As I clear out the drying vines and chop the debris for compost, I know that I have had a perfect Zen garden, successes and failures included. My year in the garden has been filled with lush foliage, brilliant color, unspeakable beauty, and incomparable peacefulness. I have lost myself in my garden, and found my true self again. I have reconnected with old friends and discovered many new ones. As I rake the bare soil and cover my perennials with dry leaves, I communicate my final message to my garden for this season: *I'll be back.*